Genealogy of the *Kings* of France and their wives

Claude Wenzler

Contents

TRANSLATION: 5/5

EDITIONS OUEST-FRANCE
13, rue du Breil, Rennes

The Great Dynasties

The Franks

The Franks entered into history in the middle of the 3rd century, in 258 at the time of the first invasions of Gaul. Fearsome warriors, they did not, however, up to the 4th century, present a united political front, since they were divided in several tribal groups. Two among them were particularly outstanding: the Salien-Franks and the Franks of the Rhine. The first, the more important, established themselves in what at present corresponds to Belgium. It was provided with its own legal code, the "Lex Saliqua" - salic law, in which one of the articles led to preventing women from acceding to the throne. The second group, less cohesive, settled in the region of Cologne, on the banks of the Rhine and Moselle. In the 8th century it took the name "Ripuarian Franks".

The conquest of Gaul by the Franks occurred imperceptibly first of all and in two ways. Firstly, the Franks, ostensibly prisoners, were hired by Rome to colonise the Gallic lands, where they gradually sowed their culture. Secondly, from the end of the 3rd century, Frankish soldiers were enrolled in the Roman legions, first of all in the auxiliary corps, then in the campaigning armies. Subsequently they became familiar with the way the empire was governed and administered. Some of them even became senior officers, such as Merobaud, nominated a « *Magister Peditum* », i.e. general, by the emperor Valentinian in 375.

Taking advantage of the weakening of Roman authority after the barbarian invasions of 406, the Franks progressively extended their domination: Clodion, from whom the Merovingians descended, conquered the north of Gaul as far as the Somme, after taking Cambrai (around 430-440). Meanwhile the Franks of the Rhine occupied the present Rhineland. Slow until the 5th century, the Frankish advance accelerated under Clovis, who undertook the submission of all the Gallic tribes.

▾ **Pharamon.**
Private collection C. Lebédel.

The Merovingians

The dynasty dates back to Pharamond, Frankish chief who died in 428 and who was a remote ancestor of Clovis. The dynasty made a discrete entry into history with Clodion (or Chlodion), called the Hairy, becoming king of Cambrai after taking control of the north of Gaul - around 430-440 - then with Merovee who, taking part with Aetius, the Roman general, in the defeat of Attila at the Catalaunic fields (451), gave his name to the first dynasty of the kings of France.

Nonetheless, the foundation of the dynasty is usually attributed to Clovis I, son of Childeric I, owing to the energy which he displayed in uniting the various Frankish peoples and keeping them under his domination. His political ability was no less remarkable: he demonstrated it, encouraged by his wife Clotilde, by having himself baptised with three thousand of his soldiers in Reims (496). He thereby became the sole Christian barbarian king. Clovis was from then on better accepted by peoples among whom Christianity was making progress; he also received episcopal support.

Reigning first of all over the Salien-Franks, the Merovingians extended their supremacy, starting from the accession of Clovis (482) and after the latter's conquests, took Gaul as a whole, where they founded a new civilisation, a mixture of Frankish, Germanic and Roman elements with Gallic and Christian components. Their hegemony was maintained in Gaul up to the taking of power by Pepin the Short (751), i.e. more than three centuries.

On the death of Clovis (511), his conquests were divided between his four sons, Thierry I, Clodomir, Childebert I and Clotaire I, who continued his expansion policy by annexing the Burgundian kingdom (534) and winning Provence (537). Overcoming rivalries, escaping assassination and taking advantage of death through natural causes, Clotaire for a short while

Partition of the Frankish Kingdom (561).

▼ **Baptism of Clovis in Reims (496).**
By receiving holy unction, Clovis enters into history as the first barbarian Christian king.
Versailles and Trianon palaces.
Photo RMN - Gérard Blot.

re-established the unity of the « *Regnum Francorum* » (558) His death (561) caused a further dismembering of the kingdom between his sons: Caribert became king of Paris (561 to 567), Gontrand king of Burgundy (561 to 593), Sigebert received Austrasia, i.e. the east of present-day France (561 to 575) and Chilperic I the kingdom of Soissons (561 to 584). This partition unleashed further rivalries, conflicts and bloodshed.

Although Dagobert, king from 629 to 639, managed to re-establish a strong and stable sovereignty, his sons Sigebert III, king of Austrasia and Clovis II, king of Burgundy and Neustria - northern France - once more tore it apart. They abandoned power to the kingdom's great dignitaries, and in particular the Mayors of the Palace - who were originally major-domos in charge of the management of the royal household. First of all it was Pepin d'Héristal who, in his capacity as mayor, imposed his authority from 679. Subsequently his descendants governed all the « *Regnum Francorum* » under the nominal reign of the « *fainéants* » (do nothing) kings - Clovis III, Childebert III, Dagobert III, Chilperic II, Clotaire IV and Thierry IV. Using the power conferred upon him and with the agreement of Pope Zacharias, Pepin the Short, son of Charles Martel, confined Childeric III, the last Merovingian king, to a monastery and took possession of the royal title (751), giving birth to the Carolingian dynasty.

▲ **Pepin the Short. Recumbent statue.**
Saint-Denis Abbey. Photo Hervé Champollion.

The Carolingians

Descending from the Pippinides - from the name of Pepin de Landen, grandfather of Pepin d'Héristal - this Frankish family gradually replaced the fading Merovingians. Pepin the Short, after gaining royal power (751), was crowned by the Pope in Soissons (752) then at Saint-Denis (754). The alliance between the royalty and the church strengthened the power of the Carolingians: sustained by Rome, Pepin the Short then Charlemagne were able to start an energetic expansion policy, both for the "Regnum Francorum" and Christianity.

The Carolingian expansion started around 755, when Pepin the Short reacted to an appeal from Pope Etienne II whose interests were threatened by the Lombards. It continued under his son Charles, the future Charlemagne, who campaigned in Germany, Spain and Italy to overcome the Lombard kingdom. The campaigns largely completed by the end of the 8th century, considerable prestige was conferred on Charles: sole possessor of temporal power throughout Christianity, he was crowned « *Emperor of the Romans* », in Rome (800), thereby confirming the union of the Empire with the Papacy. Nonetheless, the empire's power remained fragile. Bearing in mind the diversity of states which it comprised, a strong personality, like that of Charlemagne, was necessary to maintain unity. Unfortunately, the weakness of Louis I the Pious, his son, rendered the unity dangerously fragile all the more so since Frankish law, dividing succession between the male heirs, still prevailed.

By virtue of this law, from 806 onwards Charlemagne, by the act of Thionville, had provided for the partition of his empire between his three sons. But death, which struck Pepin in 810 and Charles in 813, left Louis I the Pious the sole inheritor. Consequently in the latter's case, the empire was not divided: he also promulgated

the « *Ordinatio Imperii* » (817) proclaiming, despite ancient customs, Lothaire his oldest son, sole beneficiary of the imperial dignity and sole inheritor of the Empire. He immediately associated him with power. The idea, however, was too new, too strongly opposed to the erstwhile custom of partition, to be accepted: instead of preserving the Empire's unity, it started a dynastic quarrel, which proved fatal. The entire reign of Louis I was therefore troubled by rebellions and rivalries between his sons Lothaire, Pepin, Louis the Germanic and Charles the Bald. These continued after his death, and resulted in the Treaty of Verdun (843), dividing the Empire into three kingdoms, attributed to Lothaire, Louis and Charles.

The Carolingian form of government proved to be weak: ineffectual administration, in the hands of friends or relations, and the oral transmission of imperial orders gave rise to the birth of a powerful feudalism. Also, at each successive partition, the dismemberment of the kingdoms led the Occident towards a territorial patchwork.

From the cultural point of view, on the other hand, the Carolingian period provided a veritable explosion of the arts in many fields - frescoes, illuminated manuscripts, architecture, sculpture in ivory, etc. Its influence was still distinctly perceptible at the end of the 10th century.

▲ **Battle of Fontenoye-en-Puisaye (840).**
Louis the Germanic and Charles the Bald versus Lothaire, rivals for the succession to Louis the Pious, their father.
Versailles and Trianon palaces.
Photo RMN - Gérard Blot.

Charlemagne's empire (800)

The Capetians

The Capetian dynasty, which was the true founder of royal power in France, reigned for nearly eight centuries, originally in the direct line from 987 to 1328 and subsequently through collateral branches. The main branch owes its names to Hugh Capet, coming from the Robertiens, a family which played an important role starting from Robert the Strong, who died in 866 having become famous for fighting the Normans and whose sons Eudes and Robert I reigned in France respectively from 888 to 898 and 922 to 923, alternating with the Carolingians. Hugh Capet's succession to the throne, at the death of Louis V, the last Carolingian, amounted to the real beginning of the history of the Capetian house. It finished, however, with Charles IV the Fair, who died without male heir. His brothers Louis X and Louis V having died, his sister Isabelle being denied the throne by virtue of the salic law excluding women from succession, the crown then passed to his son Philip VI of Valois.

Coming from a modest domain in Ile-de-France in 987, the Capetians managed to extend their kingdom in a remarkable way: on the death of the last Capetian king, Charles IV the Fair (1328), only Flanders, Brittany and Burgundy remained outside their kingdom, whose eastern frontiers approximately followed the courses of the Escaut, Meuse and Rhone. Philip Augustus even managed to eliminate the large enclave formed by the Plantagenets' domain in the western provinces - the struggle against the English, moreover, remained one of the priorities of the Capetian reign.

The royal domain in the 12th century.

Expansion on this scale was not feasible without the support of an effective administration: the Capetians were determined to assert their authority over all their subjects and centralise their power. They made the great feudal lords, whose suzerains they were, accustomed to bow before the royal power, for example by intervening in their lands. They also knew how to create new institutions, such as the Council of the King, Parliament and the Chamber of Accounts, etc. enabling the kingdom gradually to escape from the feudal grip and exist as a State. Probably their greatest ability was to take advantage of certain usages, such as the one which governed the succession: originally, it was the rule of election to the crown which prevailed. To avoid the crown escaping from their descendants, the Capetians ensured their succession by associating their eldest sons with power who, generally,

◄ **Suger, abbot of Saint-Denis, confers the standard of France on Louis VI the Fat, on the march against the troops of Henry V, the Holy Roman Emperor.**
Versailles and Trianon palaces. Photo RMN - Gérard Blot.

replaced them on the throne after an election in principle by the Great Lords. Subsequently, little by little, they succeeded in imposing the hereditary principle, guaranteeing dynastic continuity by crowning, while still alive, the chosen successor.
In religious matters, the Capetians enjoyed great prestige. They gave favours to churches and abbeys, taking clerics as advisers - the famous Suger, abbot of Saint-Denis, was the adviser of Louis VI and Louis VII. In return the royal power, having become hereditary, was also consecrated, which invested the king with an aura of divine right. In addition, from Philip I, who acceded to the throne in 1060, the king even had the reputation of healing by touch illnesses such as scrofula... In the case of Saint Louis, he was, for Christianity as a whole, the living model of a Christian king and his canonisation (1297) further increased the dynasty's prestige.

The Valois

The house of Valois reigned in France from the accession of Philip VI (1328) to that of Henri IV (1589). Cadet line of the Capetian dynasty, itself it had three branches:

• The **direct Valois**, descended from Charles de Valois, younger brother of Philip IV the Fair, who reigned from the accession to the throne of Philip VI (1328) until the death without heirs of Charles VIII (1498).

• The **Valois-Orléans**, descended from Louis I of Orléans, second son of Charles V. Louis XII is the only representative of this branch to ascend the throne (1498 to 1515).

• The **Valois-Angoulême**, descended from Louis I of Angoulême, who acceded to the crown on the death of Louis XII, with François I (1515). They kept it up to the death without descendants of Henri III (1589).

From the time of their accession to the throne, the House of Valois faced the tests of the Hundred Years War: defeats and English occupation of a part of the kingdom diminished their authority, the great feudal lords contested their sovereignty, dangerously threatened by the division of the country into the opposing factions of Armagnacs and Burgundians. The legendary epic of Joan of Arc (1429), however, revived patriotic sentiment, which enabled Charles VII to repulse the English invader.
Nonetheless, from the end of the 15th century, the Valois (including Charles VII and Louis XI), managed to impose their sovereignty on the great feudal lords and by improving the institutions, they ensured the centralisation of power. Their end was approaching, however, hastened by the Italian Wars and the Wars of Religion, and also an almost constant struggle against Charles Quint, the Holy Roman Emperor. It was also the time of the splendours and refinement of the Renaissance, with Louis XII, François I and Henri II as the promoters. It was the period of Chambord, Fontainebleau, the Louvre...

Assassination of Henri IV. ▸
On 14 May 1610 the king, who had inaugurated a regime of religious tolerance with the Edict of Nantes (1598), was stabbed to death by de Ravaillac, fanatical former member of the League.
Château de Pau.
Photo RMN - H. Lewandowski.

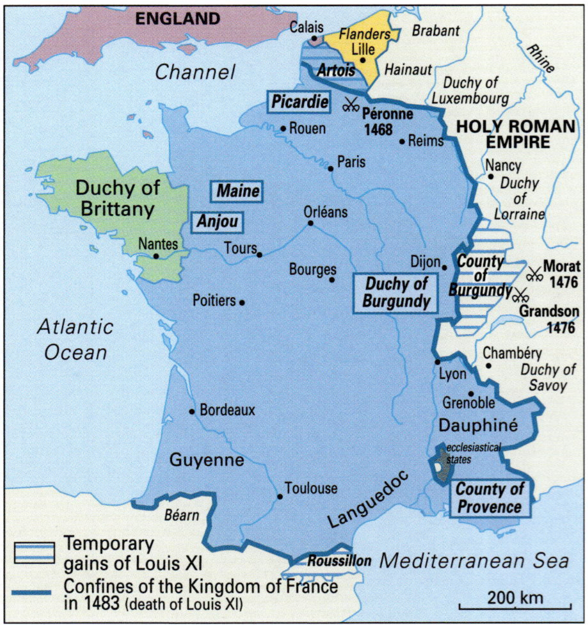

France at the death of Louis XI.

The Bourbons

The foundation of the House of Bourbon, which takes its name from Bourbon-l'Archambault, capital of the Duchy of Bourbon, dates back to the XIIIth century. It hinges on Robert de Clermont, who died in 1317, sixth son of Saint Louis and husband of Béatrice de Bourbon. Two main branches emerged from the House: the **senior branch** and the **Marche-Vendôme.**

Descended from Pierre I (1311-1356), the **senior branch** notably provided Pierre II, ruler of Beaujeu, seventh Duke of Bourbon, husband of Anne of France, regent of the kingdom with his wife during the minority of Charles VIII and also Charles III, eighth Duke of Bourbon, constable of France. He was dispossessed of his duchy in 1523 by Francis I for siding with the Empire. His fief was given to the House of Marche-Vendôme, represented by Antoine de Bourbon, died in 1562, husband of Jeanne d'Albret and father of Henri of Navarre, the future Henri IV: the latter was the first representative of the **Marche-Vendôme line - or Bourbon-Vendôme -** which from 1589 to 1830 almost continuously

▲ **Louis XIV in procession in the gardens of Versailles. In the vast palace and its immense rectangular gardens, the Court lived at the pace of the Sun King, dependent on his good will.** *Versailles and Trianon palaces.* Photo RMN - Gérard Blot.

provided the succession to the throne - Henri IV, Louis XIII, Louis XIV, Louis XV, Louis XVI, Louis XVIII and Charles X. It became extinct in 1883, with the death without posterity of the Count de Chambord at Frohsdorf.

A number of collateral branches descended from the Bourbon-l'Archambault:

• The **Condés**: this branch descended from Louis I of Bourbon, Prince of Condé and was made famous, among other things, by the Great Condé of legendary courage. It disappeared in 1804 with the Duc d'Enghien. From the branch the Conti line was born, extinct in 1814.

• The **Bourbon-Orléans**: they divided into two branches: the first confined to Gaston d'Orléans, died in 1660, brother of Louis XIII and his daughter, the "Grande Mademoiselle" who died without posterity in 1693. The second was descended from Philip, Duke of Orléans, brother of Louis XIV and reigned with Louis-Philip.

• The **Spanish Bourbons**: this branch acceded to the throne of Spain in 1700 with Philip V,

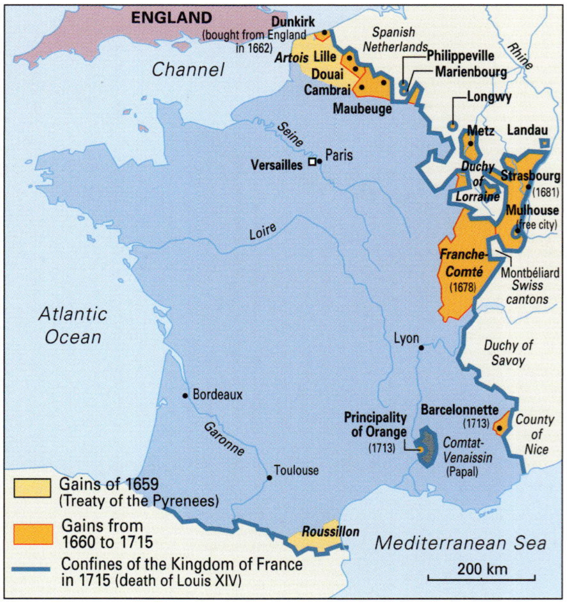

France at the death of Louis XIV (1715).

Duke of Anjou, third grandson of Louis XIV; he died in 1746. Juan Carlos, grandson of Alphonse XIII, proclaimed king of Spain (1975) on the death of General Franco, descends in a direct line from Philip V and therefore the Sun-King. The Bourbons of Spain spawned several lines, including **Bourbon-Parma**, descended from Philip, younger son of Philip V, Duke of Parma, who lost the Duchy of Parma (1860) and the **Sicilian Bourbons**, descended from Ferdinand, second son of Charles III of Spain, King of the Two Sicilies, who was also dispossessed (1860).

In the 17th century the Bourbon family raised absolute monarchy to its zenith and imposed the French supremacy on Europe, despite serious difficulties. In fact, Louis XIV was almost constantly at war internally, owing to the revolts of a people overburdened by taxation and opposition from princes of the blood, disappointed from being progressively excluded from power - the king governed with a small Council of a few faithful. Abroad, Spanish and German pretensions threatened the integrity of the kingdom.

Despite a degree of weakening of absolute monarchy, the 18th century is above all the time when the House of Bourbon occupied the thrones of France, Spain, Parma and the Two Sicilies, extending the family power as far as Italy, India and Canada.

▼ **Louis XVI at the foot of the scaffold. Condemned by a narrow majority in the Convention, the King was executed on 21 January 1793. His death unleashed the coalition of European nations against France.** *Versailles and Trianon palaces.* Photo RMN.

Kings of France

The Franks

Clodion - or Chlodion - the Hairy
(around 400 - 429 - 447)*
Frankish chief, he reigned over the Salien Franks from 429 until his death in 447.

Merovee (or Merowig)
(? - 447 - 457)
Presumed son of Clodion, he succeeded him from 447 onwards. With the Roman general Aetius he took part in the battle of the Catalaunic fields (451) which led to Attila's defeat.

Childeric I
(436 - 457 - 481)
Wife: Basine of Thuringia.
Last pagan king, he succeeded his father Merovee in 457.

The Merovingians

Clovis
(465 - 481 - Paris 511)
Wife: Clotilde.
Son of Childeric I and Basine, at Soissons (486) he beat the Roman general Syagrius, who was commanding the Roman troops in Gaul. The decisive victory delivered him, either by conquest or by capitulation, all the country north of the Loire. He then fought the Alamans at Tolbiac (496), then overcame the king of the Burgundians Gontebaud in 500, near Dijon, and the king of the Visigoths, Alaric III, in 507, at Vouillé.

On his death, almost all the Gallic tribes, with the exception of those in the Rhone basin and the Mediterranean regions, ranked under his authority.
Under pressure from his wife Clotilde, Burgundian princess, he adopted Catholicism, the religion of the great majority of his subjects; he was baptised in Rome at Christmas 496, by Saint Remi. Clovis was then supported by the episcopate. Following Frankish succession law, his kingdom was divided between his four sons.

▼ **Clovis.**
Private collection C. Lebédel.

Clotaire I the Old
(497 - 558 - Compiègne 561)
Wives: Chunsène, Gondioque, Ingone, Arégonde, Radegonde, Vultrade.
Last son of Clovis, he reconquered his brothers' lands. On his death, the kingdom was once more divided between his four sons.

Clotaire II the Young
(584 - 613 - 629)
Wives: Haldetrude, Bertrude, Sichilde - or Sicheut.
Son of the king of Neustria Chilperic I (523-584) and Fredegonda, he was king of the Franks from 613 to 629.

* Note: the three years shown correspond to the year of birth, accession to the throne and death.

THE FRANKS AND THE MEROVINGIANS

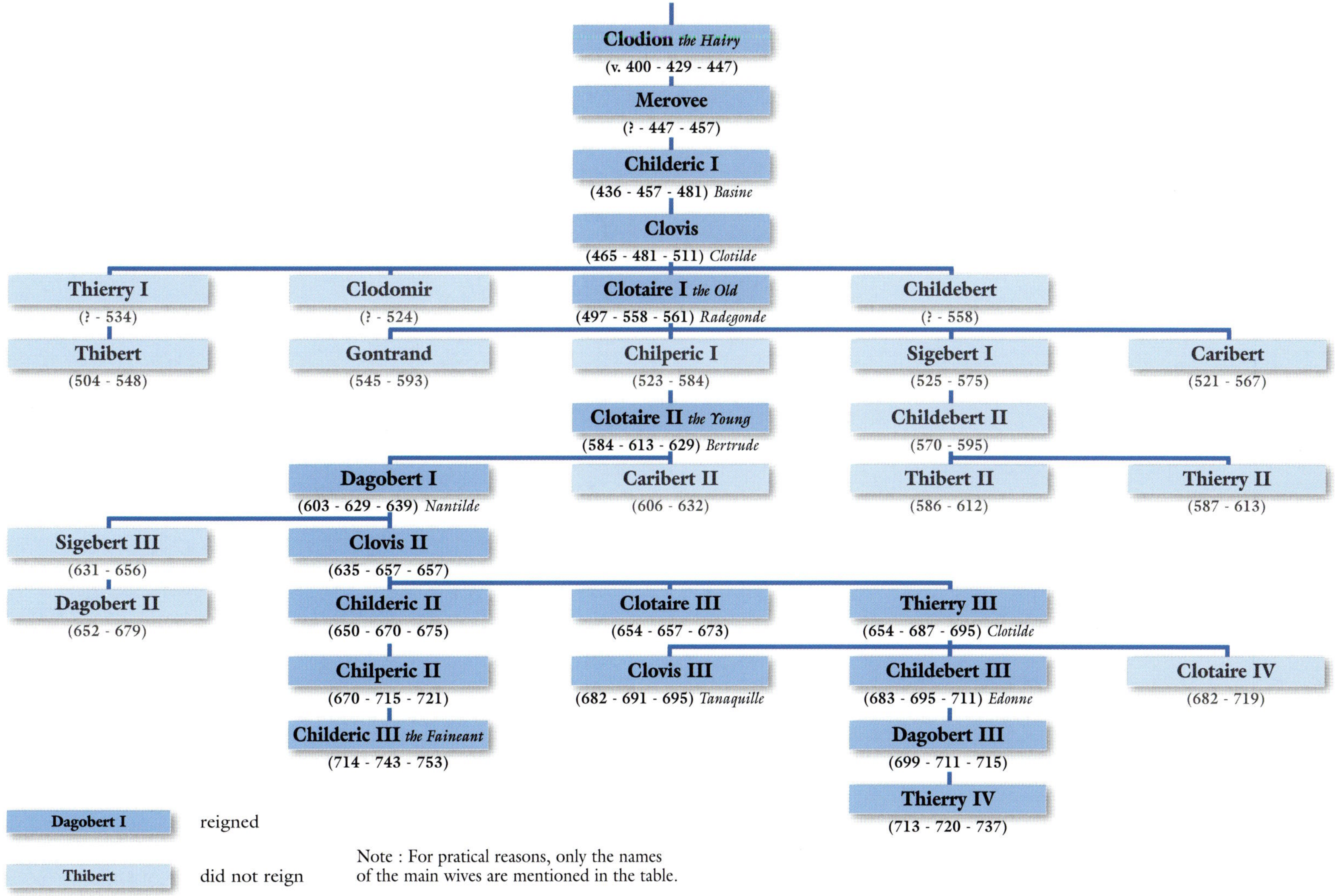

Note : For pratical reasons, only the names of the main wives are mentioned in the table.

Dagobert. ▸
Private collection
C. Lebédel.

Dagobert I
(603 - 629 - Saint-Denis 639)
Wives: Gomotrude, Nanthilde, Ragnetrude.
Son of Clotaire II and Bertrude, he was designated, while his father was alive, king of Austrasia, at the command of Pepin de Landen, Mayor of the Palace, around 623 and became the sole king of the Franks in 629.
For more than ten years, surrounded by enlightened advisers - Saint Ouen and Saint Eloi - he re-established the unity of the « *Regnum Francorum* » and restored royal authority. He was, moreover, one of the rare Merovingians to reign without partition, his personal prestige ensuring him the absolute submission of his kingdom.

Clovis II
(635 - 657 - 657)
Wife: Bathilda.
Became king of all the country in 657, he left his mother and the Mayors of the Palace to govern.

Clotaire III
(654 - 657 - 673)
First son of Clovis II and Bathilda, he left the Mayor of the Palace to govern.

Childeric II
(650 - 670 - 675)
Wife: Bilichilde.
Second son of Clovis II, he too allowed the Mayor of the Palace to rule in his place. He was assassinated while hunting in the forest of Bondy.

Thierry III
(654 - 687 - 695)
Wife: Clotilde.
His reign was disturbed by internal struggles and rivalry for power during which the Mayors of the Palace frequently intervened.

Clovis III
(682 - 691 - 695)
Wife: Tanaquille
Son of Thierry III and Clotilde, he only had the semblance of reigning, because Pepin of Heristal held power. He died without posterity.

Childebert III
(683 - 695 - 711)
Wife: Edonne.
Son of Thierry III, dominated by Pepin d'Heristal, the Mayor the Palace to whom he abandoned all power, he was the very image of the « *roi fainéant* » (do-nothing king).

Dagobert III
(699 - 711 - 715)
Son of Childebert III, he left Pepin d'Heristal to govern in his name.

Chilperic II
(670 - 715 - 721)
Son of Childeric II, he was first of all protected by his Mayor of the Palace, Charles Martel, who abandoned him by recognising as king Clotaire IV, presumed son of Thierry III.

Thierry IV of Chelles
(713 - 720 - 737)
Son of Dagobert III, he governed under the command of Charles Martel, who took him from the Abbey of Chelles where he was brought up.

Childeric III the Fainéant
(714 - 743 - Saint-Bertin - near Saint-Omer 753)
Wife: Gisele.
Son of Chilperic II, chosen by Charles Martel to succeed Thierry IV, he was crowned in 743 by Pepin the Short, Mayor of the Palace, but his power was only a façade and, deposed by Pepin in 751, he was confined to a monastery close to Saint-Omer, while his son was relegated to the abbey of Saint-Wandrille.

▾ **Pepin the Short.**
Private collection
C. Lebédel.

THE CAROLINGIANS

Pepin the Elder
(v. 580 - 640)

Ansegisel
(? - 679)

Pepin d'Héristal
(v. 640 - 714)

Charles Martel
(685 - 741)

Pepin the Short
(715 - 751 - 768) *Bertha*

Charlemagne
(742 - 768 - 814) *Hildegarde*

Carloman
(751 - 768 - 771)

Charles
(? - 813)

Louis I *the Debonnaire or Pious*
(778 - 814 - 840) *Ermangarde, Judith of Bavaria*

Pepin
(806 - 810)

Louis the Germanic
(804 - 843)

Lothaire I
(795 - 855)

Pepin of Aquitaine
(803 - 838)

Charles II *the Bald*
(823 - 840 - 877) *Ermentrude*

Charles the Fat
(839 - 884 - 888) *Richarde*

Louis II *the Stammerer*
(846 - 877 - 879) *Ansgarde d'Hiémois, Adélaïde of Paris*

Carloman
(866 - 879 - 884)

Louis III
(863 - 879 - 882)

Charles III *the Simple*
(879 - 898 - 929) *Odgive of England*

Louis IV *of Outremer*
(918 - 936 - 954) *Gerberge of Saxony*

Lothaire
(941 - 954 - 986) *Emma*

Louis V *the Faineant*
(967 - 986 - 987) *Adélaïde of Anjou*

Charlemagne reigned

Charles did not reign

Note : For pratical reasons, only the names of the main wives are mentioned in the table.

The Carolingians

Pepin the Short

(Jupille (Belgium) 715 - 751 - Saint-Denis 768)

Wives: Rotrude - or Chotrud, Swanahilde - or Sonichilde, Bertha, called the Big Foot - or Bertrade de Laon.

Second son of Charles Martel and Rotrude, he succeeded his father in 741 alongside his brother Carloman, Mayor of the Palace. After the abdication of Carloman in 747, Pepin the Short in 750 requested the support of Pope Zacharius to depose the Merovingian Childeric III: he obtained the famous reply, according to which it was the king who really exercised power. Childeric III was therefore sent to a monastery in 751 and Pepin was proclaimed king. Crowned at Soissons (752) then at Saint-Denis (754), he from then on benefited from the legitimacy acquired by Clovis I, of being God's elect. The alliance between the crown and the Holy See was reflected from 754 and 756 by two campaigns in Italy during which Pepin gave assistance to Pope Etienne II, threatened by the king of the Lombards Aistulf. Also, he was the conqueror of Aquitaine (760-768) and died after dividing his kingdom between his two sons.

▲ **Charlemagne.**
Palais de Justice, Paris. Photo Hervé Champollion.

Charles I the Great - or Charlemagne

(from the Latin *Carolus Magnus*)
(742 - 768 - Aix-la-Chapelle 814)
Wives: Himiltrude, Desirade, Hildegarde, Fastrade, Liutgarde, Madelgarde, Gerswinde, Regina, Adelinde.
Eldest son of Pepin the Short and Berthe, crowned king in 751, he reigned first of all over Aquitaine, Neustria, Austrasia and his Germanic dependencies, then in 771 he inherited the possessions of his elder brother Carloman. Unity of the « *Regnum Francorum* » thereby re-established, Pope Leon III crowned him Emperor of the Romans, on Christmas day 800 in Rome.
Installed in Aix-la-Chapelle, the most prestigious of the Carolingian sovereigns, throughout his long reign he pursued two main ambitions. The first was the re-establishment of order. He conferred on counts and bishops lands for which they took direct responsibility, controlled by *missi dominici* which maintained contact between the palace and the local administration. To govern more effectively, he replaced orders, up to then oral, by written decrees - *capitulaires*. He reformed justice, created a corps of specialised judges nominated by the *missi*. To provide himself with the support of a strong church, he associated bishops and abbots in secular administration, without depriving himself of the authority to intervene in ecclesiastical affairs, nor from supervising the spiritual and moral recovery of order among the clergy and the faithful. He organised the spread of the gospel in newly conquered regions, Christian education of children and the instruction of clerics. As a result a very large number of schools and monasteries were founded during his reign. His policy revived intellectual and artistic activity, which has come to be called the "Carolingian Renaissance".
His second ambition was to build a widespread Christian empire in the Occident. He directed many military campaigns: in Lombardy (774), against the Saxons, submitted in 804, against the Arabs in Spain in 778, against the Bavarians, the Avars in Hungary (791-796)... At the end of the 8th century his empire was immense, occupying most of the Occident, but it proved short-lived because by the act of Thionville (806) while living, he divided it among his three sons.

Louis I the Debonnair or Pious

(Chasseneuil 778 - 814 - near Ingelheim 840)
Wives: Irmingarde (or Ermangarde), Judith of Bavaria.
Third son of Charlemagne and Hildegarde, he was in 781 king of Aquitaine, then on the death of his brothers, he became the sole successor of Charlemagne, who crowned him Emperor at Aix-la-Chapelle in 814. In order to settle his succession in advance, while living he divided the empire into three kingdoms, granted to each one of his sons, Louis the Germanic, Pepin of Aquitaine and Lothaire, with primacy for the latter, the elder - *Ordinatio Imperii*, 817. The act was a compromise between the idea of the unity of the empire and the Frank custom of divided succession.
But the second wife of Louis the Pious, Judith of Bavaria in 823 gave birth to a fourth son, Charles, and requesting that he be endowed in the same way as his brothers, rejected the division of 817. A serious crisis arose, during which the four sons rebelled against their father. Finally, Charlemagne's immense empire was partitioned after the death of Pepin of Aquitaine, between Louis the Germanic, Charles and Lothaire (treaty of Verdun, 843).

Charles II the Bald

(Frankfurt 823 - 840 - Avrieux 877)
Wives: Ermentrude, Richeut.
Younger son of Louis I the Pious and Judith of Bavaria, he was impassioned by the arts, letters, arguments and theology and made his court a brilliant centre of culture.
His reign, however, was disturbed: he had to confront the jealousy of his brothers, Lothaire, Louis the Germanic, and Pepin of Aquitaine, born from a first marriage of his father and beneficiaries of the partition of the empire in 817 - *Ordinatio Imperii*. After the treaty of Verdun in 843, he obtained a large part of the empire, became King of France in 843, and was crowned Emperor of the Romans in 875 by Pope John VIII.

Louis II the Stammerer

(846 - 877 - Compiègne 879)
Wives: Ansgarde d'Hiémois, Adélaïde - or Aélis - of Paris.
Son of Charles II the Bald and Ermentrude, he revolted against his father and was with difficulty recognised as king in 877. During his reign, the kingdom weakened into multiple lordships.

Louis III and Carloman

(Louis : 863 - 879 - Saint-Denis 882
Carloman : 866 - 879 - 887)
Sons of Louis II the Stammerer and Ansgarde, Louis III and Carloman reigned jointly and confronted the Normans on the Loire and in Normandy. On the death of Louis III, Carloman reigned alone.

Charles the Fat

(Neidingen 839 - 884 - Neidingen 888)
Wife: Richarde.
Son of Louis the Germanic, grandson of Louis the Debonair, he became King of France in 884 to the detriment of Charles the Simple; he took part, without opposing it, in the siege of Paris by the Normans in 885. Withdrawn to Alsace, he was deposed at the Diet of Tribur (November 887) and took refuge in the monastery of Reichenau in Swabia where he died the following year.

Eudes

(860 - 888 - La Fère 898)
Wife: Theoderada.
He was not a Carolingian: eldest son of Robert the Strong, in reality he was a Robertien, the branch from which the Capetians descended. Count of Paris, in 885 he successfully defended the town and repulsed the Norman siege despite the king's inertia. In 888, the Great Lords crowned him in Compiègne. He had to face the Carolingian Charles the Simple, who the Archbishop of Reims had already crowned in 893. After a confused struggle, Eudes, ill, treated with the latter in 897 and died the following year, having recommended that his vassals recognise his former rival.

Charles III the Simple

(879 - 898 - Péronne 929)
Wife: Odgive - or Edvige - of England.
Posthumous son of Louis II the Stammerer and Adelaide, his rights were contested. Crowned in Reims in 893, he first of all shared power with Eudes (896 to 898), then reigned alone from 898 to 923. He negotiated peace with Rollon, the Norman chief - treaty of Saint-Clair-sur-Epte, 911 - authorising their settlement in the valley of the Seine and thereby putting an end

to the Viking invasions into the Frankish kingdom. His legitimacy was contested by Duke Robert - brother of the defunct king Eudes - who crowned in Reims (922), was attacked near Soissons by Charles III; he was killed in 923, whereas Charles, defeated, had to flee. Subsequently, Charles caught in an ambush in Château-Thierry, was imprisoned in Peronne where he died; his wife went into exile in England, taking with her their son, the future Louis IV of Outremer.

Robert I

(860 - 922 - Soissons 923)
Wife: Beatrice de Vermandois.
His offices and titles were confirmed by Charles the Simple, who also granted him the suzerainty of Burgundy. He fought the Normans, then rebelled against the king (920). Crowned in Reims in 922, he was attacked near Soissons by Charles the Simple; he was killed, whereas the king, defeated, had to flee.
He was not a Carolingian, but a Robertien, second son of Robert the Strong, whose eldest son Eudes had already reigned from 888 to 898.

Raul - or Rodolphe

(? - 923 - Auxerre 936)
Wife: Emma.
Son of Richard, Duke of Aquitaine and son-in-law of Robert I - neither was he a true Carolingian - he succeeded his father-in-law with the agreement of the latter's son, Hugh the White. He fought the Hungarians, the Germanics, the Normans and died without heir.

Louis IV of Outremer

(918 - 936 - Reims 954)
Wife: Gerberge of Saxony.
After the defeat of his father Charles the Simple, his mother Odgive took him to England to his grandfather Edward. Returning to France, Louis IV had to overcome a coalition led by Hugh the White, which shook the throne: also, allied to Otto I, king of Germany and Conrad, king of Provence, he took possession of Reims, whereas the Pope excommunicated Hugh in 948. His authority was thereby re-established.

Lothaire

(Reims 941 - 954 - Reims 986)
Wife: Emma.
He was the son of Louis IV and Gerberge of Saxony. During his minority, the Bishop of Cologne directed the kingdom. Lothaire's policy caused Otto II to invade Lorraine, whom he repulsed, aided by Hugh Capet in 978. Otto II having died in 983, he took advantage of Otto III's young age (3 years) to attempt to destabilise the Germanic Holy Roman Empire.

Louis V le Fainéant

(967 - 986 - Compiègne 987)
Wife: Adelaide of Anjou.
Son of Lothaire, he was associated with the throne in 978 and was called « *le Fainéant* ».- the "Do-nothing" for no reason. He was besieging Reims, as a result of a conspiracy by Archbishop Adalbéron, when he died following a hunting accident in the Forest of Compiègne. Without heir, he was replaced on the throne by Hugh Capet.

▼ **Hugh Capet.**
Private collection C. Lebédel.

The Capetians

Hugh Capet

(939 - 987 - 996)
Wife: Adelaide (Aelis) of Aquitaine (or Poitou).
Elder son of Hugh the Great, Count of Paris, Hugh Capet was descended from the Robertien family, who for a century dominated Francia - comprising the region between the Meuse and the Loire. It had already provided two kings - Eudes and Robert I. It already possessed vast domains, numerous vassals and a famous family when he was crowned king at Noyon and consecrated at Reims (987). He associated his son Robert with power from the time of his succession to the throne, thereby creating a principle of dynastic heredity, which was to last for nearly eight centuries.

THE CAPETIANS

Bivin
(? - ?)

Richard the Lawful
(? - 921)

Raul
(? - 923 - 936) *Emma*

Robert the Strong
(825 - 866)

Eudes
(860 - 888 - 898) *Theoderada*

Robert I
(860 - 922 - 923) *Beatrice de Vermandois*

Hugh the Great
(? - 936)

Hugh Capet
(939 - 987 - 996) *Adélaïde of Aquitaine*

Robert II *the Pious*
(972 - 996 - 1031) *Berthe of Burgundy, Constance of Provence*

Hugh
(1017 - 1026)

Henri I
(1008 - 1031 - 1061) *Anne of Kiev*

Philip I
(1052 - 1060 - 1108) *Berthe of Holland, Bertrade de Montfort*

Louis VI *the Fat*
(1084 - 1108 - 1137) *Adélaïde of Savoy*

Philip
(? - 1131)

Louis VII *the Young*
(1120 - 1137 - 1180) *Eleanor of Aquitaine, Constance of Castille, Alix of Champagne*

Philip II Augustus
(1165 - 1180 - 1223) *Isabelle de Hainaut, Ingeburge of Denmark, Agnes de Meranie*

Louis VIII *the Lion*
(1187 - 1223 - 1226) *Blanche de Castille*

Louis IX *Saint Louis*
(1214 - 1226 - 1270) *Marguerite de Provence*

BOURBONS
(1589 - 1850)

Philip III *the Bold*
(1245 - 1270 - 1285) *Isabelle of Aragon, Marie de Brabant*

VALOIS
(1293 - 1589)

Philip IV *the Fair*
(1268 - 1285 - 1314) *Jeanne of Navarre*

Louis X *the Haughty*
(1289 - 1314 - 1316)
Marguerite of Burgundy, Clemence of Hungary

Jean I *Posthumous*
(1316 - 1316 - 1316)

Philip V *the Long*
(1292 - 1316 - 1322)
Jeanne of Burgundy

Charles IV *the Fair*
(1294 - 1322 - 1328)
Blanche of Burgundy, Marie of Luxembourg, Jeanne d'Evreux

Hugh Capet reigned

Hugh the Great did not reign

Note : For practical reasons, only the names of the main wives are mentioned in the table.

Charles, Duke of Lower-Lorraine and last Carolingian pretender, struggled to regain the crown. But imprisoned, he died in Orléans: from there on Hugh Capet and his son were unrivalled. However, Hugh Capet was only a feudal lord, hardly more powerful than his vassals. Numerous official acts provide the proof: they were not signed by the king or the chancellor alone, but also by powerful personages, whom the sovereign relied upon for support, but who effectively weakened his authority.

Robert II the Pious

(Orléans 972 - 996 - Melun 1031)

Wives: Suzanne (or Rosala) of Provence, Berthe of Burgundy, Constance of Provence (or Arles).

Son of Hugh Capet and Adelaide, he was associated with power from his father's coronation (987). Pope Gregory V annulled his marriage with his relative Berthe and the Council of Rome ordered separation in 998: he married again taking as his wife Constance, daughter of the Count of Provence and Arles. He attached Burgundy to the crown (1002-1016) and also the Counties of Dreux (1015) and Melun (1016). In addition, he supported the monks of Cluny in the reform of their order and severely repressed nascent heresies.

Henri I

(1008 - 1031 - Vitry-aux-Loges 1060)

Wives: Matilda, Anne of Russia (or Kiev).

Son of Robert II and Constance of Provence, he was granted authority by his father in 1027 whom he succeeded in 1031. His reign was notable for the incessant conflicts with rebel lords, many of whom showed pretensions for independence and settled in the royal domain: the Duke of Burgundy, Count of Blois, Duke of Normandy (future William the Conqueror), Duke of Brittany and the Duke of Aquitaine. Failing to assert his authority, Henri I, who associated his son Philip I with the throne from 1059 onwards, only managed to ensure the survival of the Capetian dynasty.

Philip I

(1052 - 1060 - Melun 1108)

Wives: Berthe of Holland, Bertrade de Montfort.

Son of Henri I and Anne of Russia, he was crowned in Reims in 1059 in the presence of his father. In 1092 he repudiated his wife Berthe and, in order to marry her, carried off Bertrade de Montfort, wife of the Count of Anjou, which led to several excommunications... During his reign the first crusade (1096) took place in which, however, he did not take part. On the other hand he sketched the outlines of Capetian policy: he gave solid foundations to royal power by developing his administration and limiting the power of over-mighty vassals. Following a custom from henceforth established, he associated his son Louis VI with the crown in 1098 thereby ensuring the continuity of the dynasty. He enlarged the royal domain by taking hold of the townships of Vermandois, Gâtinais, French Vexin, Viscounty of Bourges and the lordship of Dun-le-Roi.

Louis VI the Fat

(Paris 1084 - 1108 - Paris 1137)

Wives: Lucienne de Rochefort, Adelaide (or Alix or Aélix) of Savoy.

Son of Philip I and Berthe of Holland, he was granted authority in 1098 and crowned in 1108. He put an end to disorders caused by lords pillaging in the Ile-de-France, by eliminating Ebbes de Roucy (1102), Enguerrand de Coucy (1117) and Thomas de Marles (1130). For several years he fought Thibaut IV of Champagne, fearsome conspirator and attacked Henry I Beauclerc, Duke of Normandy and King of England. With Suger, abbott of Saint-Denis as minister, he asserted the king's sovereignty and enhanced the royal domain by supporting rural communities and urban municipalities. He married his eldest son Louis to Eleanor, sole daughter and heir of Aquitaine: his domain thereby extended from the Oise as far as the Pyrenees, sealing the alliance between North and South, which was to be compromised by Eleanor's remarriage to Henry II Plantagenet in 1137.

Louis VII the Young

(Paris 1120 - 1137 - Paris 1180)

Wives: Eleanor of Aquitaine, Constance of Castille, Alix (or Adèle) of Champagne.

Son of Louis VI and Adelaide of Savoy, he kept his father's ministers, including Suger, abbot of Saint-Denis, completed the submission of feudal lords in the Ile-de-France and pursued the enhancement of the royal domain. He supported the municipal movement and election of bishops devoted to his cause, granted privileges to rural communities, encouraged clearances and emancipation of serfs. Two important events mark his reign: his departure for the second Crusade (1147-1149) and his divorce from Eleanor of Aquitaine in 1152. In 1154 the latter married the Count of Anjou Henry II who, having become King of England, possessed a dangerous enclave in France - Normandy, Auvergne, Aquitaine and Guyenne.

Philippe II Augustus

(Gonesse 1165 - 1180 - Mantes 1223)

Wives: Isabelle de Hainaut, Ingeburge of Denmark, Agnès de Méranie.

Son of Louis VII and Alix of Champagne, at his coronation he was master of a prosperous but limited domain, comprising the Ile-de-France, the Orléanais and a part of Berry. The rest of the kingdom was split into a dozen fiefs over which the king had little authority, whereas those of the West and Aquitaine, the domain of Henry II Plantagenet, King of England, escaped him completely. Most of his reign was therefore notable for struggle with the House of England. He managed to restrain Henry II at the capitulation of Azay-le-Rideau in 1189, at Bouvines (1214) he broke a strong coalition combining the Counts of Boulogne, Flanders, Holland, Dukes of Lorraine, Brabant and Limburg and the Holy Roman Emperor.

Having extended the royal domain, Philip Augustus provided himself with new methods of government to back his power. Dispossessing the great feudal lords after having overcome them, he nominated men, of more modest extraction but more competent, officers in charge of representing his authority. He conferred the management of the royal treasury on the Templars, undertook a more thorough collection of his domain's revenues. His revenue enabled him to erect powerful castles - the "medieval" Louvre, Dourdan, Issoudun, Girsors, etc. Having installed the court in Paris, where archives have been kept since 1194, he provided the city with a new wall, Notre-Dame and the University; he caused the streets to be paved and encouraged trade. Although his relations with the Pope were deplorable, those with the bishops were, on the contrary, excellent. He scarcely intervened in Episcopal elections. His reign definitively asserted the royal authority.

Saint Louis. ►
Palais de Justice, Paris.
Photo Hervé Champollion.

Louis VIII the Lion

(Paris 1187 - 1223 - Montpensier in Auvergne 1226)

Wife: Blanche de Castille.

Son of Philip Augustus and Isabelle de Hainaut, he became king in 1223, without having been previously associated with power, as had been the rule since the advent of the Capetians, a sign that royal authority was solidly ensured.

During his reign, in 1226 he took part in the crusade against the Albigensians (1209 to 1229), preached by Pope Innocent III against the Cathar and Vaudois heretics in Languedoc. He campaigned against the towns and lordships which supported them, thereby preparing for the annexation of the Toulousain. Southern France becoming attached to northern France was made effective with the treaty of Meaux-Paris (1229) under the regency of Blanche de Castille, between Saint Louis and Raymond VII, Count of Toulouse.

Louis IX or Saint Louis

(Poissy 1214 - 1226 - Tunis 1270)

Wife: Marguerite de Provence.

Son of Louis VIII and Blanche de Castille (regent from 1226 to 1236), the sovereign was one of the greatest figures in our history, playing a capital role in the French monarchy. His politics were a reflection of his morality: he was the model of a Christian knight, combining sometimes excessive faith with great concern for justice, a strong sense of diplomacy

▲ **Saint Louis.**
Palais de Justice, Paris. Photo Hervé Champollion.

with exceptional energy. His wisdom and firmness earned him the respect of grandees throughout Europe.
He rationalised his government's administrative structures, created the Parliament and supervised bailiffs, seneschals and provosts in such a way that the rights of each were respected, also by royal office holders. He founded several hospitals, including the "Quinze-Vingts" for three hundred knights, in front of which Saracens had to lower their eyes, and built the Sainte-Chapelle in Paris.
He completed the conquest of Languedoc undertaken by Louis VIII, his father, with the treaty of Lorris (1243). He successfully countered a coalition led by Hugh de Lusignan and Raymond VII of Toulouse, supported by Henry III of England. At the time of the seventh crusade (1248 to 1254), he took Damiette, but suffered defeat at Mansurah in February 1250. Despite the Pope's advice, the reluctance of the lords and his mediocre health, he embarked for the eighth crusade at Aigues-Mortes and died of plague during the siege at Tunis (25 August 1270). He was canonised in 1297 by Pope Boniface VIII.

Philippe III the Bold

(Poissy 1245 - 1270 - Perpignan 1285)
Wives: Isabelle of Aragon, Marie de Brabant.
Son of Louis IX and Marguerite of Provence, he was proclaimed king under the walls of Tunis. At the death of Alphonse of Poitiers, brother of Saint Louis, he inherited Poitou, Auvergne, Saintonge, Toulousain and Albigeois. Supporting Charles of Anjou, King of Sicily, against Pierre II of Aragon, he undertook the « *Aragon crusade* », during which in 1285 he lost his fleet at Las Hormigas. He died in Perpignan, victim of an epidemic.

Philippe IV the Fair

(Fontainebleau 1268 - 1285 - Fontainebleau 1314)
Wife: Jeanne of Navarre.
Son of Philip III and Isabelle of Aragon, he showed extreme clear-sightedness in external politics by putting an end to the Aragon war undertaken by his father - treaty of Agnani in 1295.
A highly talented administrator, he continued the modernisation of the institutions undertaken by his

predecessors: the importance of the chancellery was strengthened, the Parliament's functions were specified, financial administration was reformed, treasury management, until then conferred upon the Templars, was henceforth undertaken by royal officials.

However, to overcome grave economic difficulties, he took recourse to hazardous expedients. For instance, he used alterations in the value of the currency, but these measures fell heavily on the poor and caused serious riots in Paris in 1306. He ordered persecutions against the Lombards and Jews, who played an important role in royal finances and trade, confiscating their goods and ordering expulsions and arrests. In vain he attempted to establish direct and regular taxation on capital, income or "feu" (fire, i.e. hearth) families. The taxes he levied on church goods led to serious conflict: the "Agnani revolt" in 1303 against Boniface VIII, was followed by the election of Clement V, the French Pope installed in Avignon and the arrest of the Templars in 1307 - confiscation of the Order's riches and supplication by Jacques Molay, Grand Master of the Temple in 1314.

Louis X the Haughty

(Paris 1289 - 1314 - Vincennes 1316)

Wives: Marguerite of Burgundy,
Clémence of Hungary.

Eldest son of Philip the Fair and Jeanne of Navarre, in 1305 he married Marguerite of Burgundy, the latter condemned for adultery, was imprisoned in Château-Gaillard, where she was strangled. He then remarried Clémence of Hungary.

His reign was noticeable for a difficult economic situation, which fostered strong feudal reactions. A serious famine (1315-1317) in the north of the kingdom accelerated the rise in prices, leading to general discontent whilst the lesser nobility, ruined, resented officials trampling on their rights, whittling away their power and resources. The Great Lords, led by Charles de Valois, uncle of Louis X, hostile to Philip the Fair's methods of government, wanted once more to direct his country's affairs.

Louis X's reign finished with a serious succession problem. The king from his first marriage produced a daughter, Jeanne, but no male heir. Jean I, called the Posthumous, was born from his second marriage, but only lived for a few days. Therefore the problem of the succession arose.

Jean I Posthumous

(Paris 1316 - 1316 - Paris 1316)

Son of Louis X and Clemence of Hungary, he was born on 15 November 1316, five months after the death of his father and died on 19 November, aged 5 days. His uncle, Philip, Count of Poitou, exercising the regency before his birth, is strongly suspected of having caused the infant's death in order to

▼ From left to right, Philip III, Philip IV and Louis X. Recumbent statues.
Saint-Denis Abbey.
Photos Hervé Champollion.

▲ **From left to right, Philip V and Charles IV. Recumbent statues.**
Saint-Denis Abbey.
Photos Hervé Champollion.

reign in his place. Moreover, he succeeded him under the name of Philip V in January 1317.

Philip V the Long

(Paris 1293 - 1316 - Longchamp 1322)
Wife: Jeanne of Burgundy.
Second son of Philip IV the Fair and Jeanne de Navarre, brother of Louis X, he carried on the regency before the birth of his nephew Jean I, who only lived five days. He ascended the throne on the latter's death, depriving his niece Jeanne, older than him, of the succession… Remarkable administrator with a strong sense of power, he continued Philip the Fair's policy, attempting to impose a common currency throughout the kingdom despite the opposition of southern lords. He centralised the institutions for more effectiveness, reorganising the Hôtel du Roi, the Parliament, the Chamber of Accounts… The economic crisis which Louis X had to face abated with difficulty and the country underwent misery, famine, revolt, such as those of the « *pastourals* » - peasants who had undertaken a crusade to the Holy Land - violent repression of Jews and lepers, usual scapegoats in similar circumstances.

Charles IV the Fair

(Clermont 1294 - 1322 - Vincennes 1328)
Wives: Blanche of Burgundy, Marie of Luxembourg, Jeanne d'Evreux.
Third son of Philip IV the Fair and Jeanne of Navarre, he succeeded Philip V, his brother, owing to the 1316 decision, which had definitely endorsed the principle of excluding women from the crown of France, he was without heir.
During his reign, he maintained the royal domination over the nobles, continued the strengthening of the administration, supervised the officials of the Chambers of Account, the Parliament, the Requests, the Chancellery and reformed their offices. Like his predecessors, he had to face incessant financial problems and had recourse to expedients of every kind: taxes on merchandise, confiscation of the goods of Italian bankers, used supposedly to finance the crusades…
He died without male descendants and was the last king on the throne from the direct Capetian dynasty.

The Valois

Philip VI

(1293 - 1328 Nogent-le-Roi 1350)

Wives: Jeanne de Bourbon (or Burgundy), Blanche of Navarre.

Son of Charles de Valois and Marguerite of Sicily, during his reign the Hundred Years War broke out while a serious economic crisis and the Great Plague struck the country. Confronted with financial difficulties, he summoned the States General (1346-1347) and instituted a new tax on salt (gabelle)... Despite difficult circumstances, the royal domain grew with the inclusion of Champagne and Brie, Montpellier and Dauphiné.

▼ **Philip VI de Valois.**
Versailles and Trianon palaces. Photo RMN - Gérard Blot.

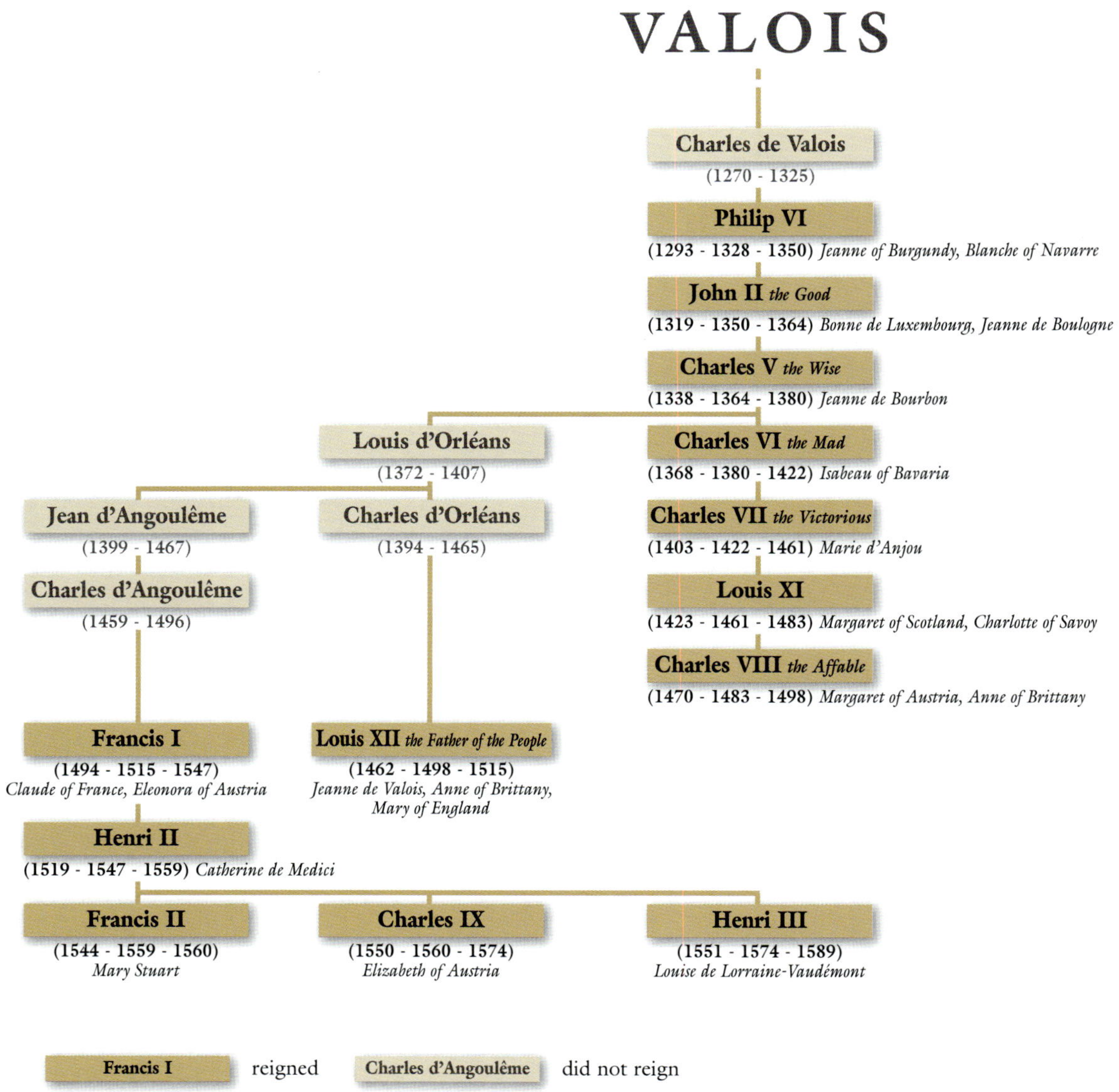

John II the Good

(Château du Gué de Maulny near Le Mans 1319 - 1350 - London 1364)

Wives: Bonne de Luxembourg - or Auvergne, Jeanne de Boulogne - or Auvergne.

Eldest son of Philip VI and Jeanne of Burgundy, his extravagance provoked remonstrances from the provincial estates which refused him the necessary resources for government ... He proved hesitant or clumsy in his political choices, meddled with the most influential lineages of the kingdom by summarily executing the constable Raoul de Brienne (1350), provoked the animosity of his cousin Charles the Bad, King of Navarre, and humiliated his own son Charles Duke of Normandy, arresting Charles the Bad when the latter was the guest of the former in Rouen...

Taken prisoner by the English in Poitiers in 1356 in a conflict with Philip of Navarre - brother of Charles the Bad, in London in 1359 he signed a treaty freeing himself at the price of a heavy ransom which was refused by the estates of Paris. His liberation therefore had to be renegotiated at the treaty of Brétigny (1360): he was able to return to France by leaving his son the Duke Louis of Anjou as hostage. But the latter fled, breaking his parole, and the king had to return to London where he died.

▲ **Charles V**
Gallery of the Famous – Château de Beauregard.
Photo Hervé Champollion.

Charles V the Wise

(Vincennes 1338 - 1364 - Nogent-sur-Marne 1380)
Wife: Jeanne de Bourbon.
He was the eldest son of Jean II the Good and Bonne of Luxembourg. After the defeat at Poitiers in 1356, his father remaining a prisoner of the English, he undertook the regency, suffering a deplorable political, economic and social situation during which he had to confront the political pretensions of the states general, a Parisian rebellion led by the provost of the merchants, Etienne Marcel, a peasant revolt in the Ile-de-France against proprietors and creditors and the constant hostility of the King of Navarre.
He obtained the liberation of his father at the treaty of Brétigny in 1360. The respite procured by the treaty and the recovery of finances enabling the king to equip himself with artillery and warships, he reorganised his army and restored town walls and royal fortresses. At the head of his army, he placed captains from the lesser nobility, such as the Breton Betrand Duguesclin with whom he imposed peace on Charles the Bad. He pacified the country, eliminating the Great Companies, bands of brigands who were formerly the troops engaged for a campaign and obliged in time of peace to live by violence and looting. On his death, only the towns of Calais, Cherbourg, Brest, Bordeaux and Bayonne remained in English hands.
Defying the princes and the great feudal lords, he surrounded himself above all with townspeople, lesser provincial lords and clerics, whose competence and wisdom restored much prestige to the crown.

Charles VI the Mad or Beloved

(Paris 1368 - 1380 - Paris 1422)
Wife: Isabeau of Bavaria.
Elder son of Charles V and Jeannne de Bourbon, he was not really able to govern since his uncles, the Dukes of Burgundy, Berry, Bourbon and Anjou held power up to 1388 and took maximum advantage of it. Reaching majority in 1388, he removed the latter and recalled to government the former advisers of his father - the « *Marmousets* ». But becoming a victim of his first bout of madness in 1392, Charles

▼ **Charles VI. Recumbent statue.**
Saint-Denis Abbey.
Photo Hervé Champollion.

allowed the Dukes of Burgundy and Berry and the Duke of Orleans, his brother, once more to dispute power. In 1407, Jean without Fear, the Duke of Burgundy having ordered the assassination of the Duke of Orléans, who had taken the regency, started a civil war between the Armagnacs and Burgundians. Henry V, King of England took the opportunity to inflict on France the defeat of Agincourt (1415). Jean without Fear having been assassinated when attempting reconciliation with the Armagnacs, the new Duke of Burgundy, Philip the Good, signed the treaty of Troyes (1420) with England, delivering France to the English - Henry V of England was to become King of France on the death of Charles VI whose daughter he was to marry. Charles VI the Mad died relegated to the Hotel Saint-Pol in 1422.

Charles VII the Victorious

(Paris 1403 - 1422 - Mehun-sur-Yèvre 1461)
Wife: Marie d'Anjou.
Son of Charles VI and Isabeau of Bavaria, he was recognised King of France only by the Armagnacs, Henry VI of England having been proclaimed King of France at the death of his father Henry V in 1422. Seeking refuge in Touraine - at Loches and Chinon and in Berry, the « *little king of Bourges* » saw most of his kingdom dominated by the English. Joan of Arc delivered Orléans and crowned the king at Reims (1429): the people saw it as a judgement of God, recognising the legitimacy of Charles VII. The idea of the nation was born in the kingdom. A methodical re-conquest was then undertaken to free the country from English garrisons.
Charles VII firmly re-established the financial institutions with the assistance of his great financier, Jacques Cœur. He succeeded in imposing on his subjects a permanent tax, which enabled him to modernise and maintain an army in time of peace as in time of war. Despite everything, Charles VII, even though he repressed a feudal rebellion, the *Praguerie* (1440), remained a king susceptible to influence, often dominated by his favourites Richemont, La Trémoille and Brézé and also by his mistress, Agnès Sorel... Owing to painful memories of his youth in Paris, he conferred the command of the capital on royal officers and continued to prefer his châteaux of Touraine and Berry.

Louis XI

(Bourges 1423 - 1461 - Plessis-lez-Tours 1483)
Wives: Margaret of Scotland, Charlotte of Savoy.
Son of Charles VII and Marie d'Anjou, he took part in the *Praguerie* against his father, whose trust however he regained. He took Dieppe from the English (1443), gained possession of the county of Armagnac (1444), but once more attracted the distrust of his father owing to his hostility to Agnès Sorel and her intrigues. Ascending the throne in 1461, he dismissed his father's advisers and attempted to break the power of the nobility. He took advantage of the death of Charles the Bold (1477) to gain Burgundy and Picardy for the crown. Reputedly a cruel, superstitious and machiavellian sovereign, he was known for his excessive severity - imprisonment of cardinal La Ballue, executions of the Count of Armagnac and the Constable of Saint-Paul. Aware that prosperity supports the power of the state, he saw to the recovery of finances, developed industry and trade, introduced new economic activities in France - such as silk in Lyon and Tours -

◂ **Charles VII.**
Gallery of the Famous – Château de Beauregard.
Photo Hervé Champollion.

▼ **Louis XI.**
Private collection
C. Lebédel.

▲ **Charles VIII.**
Gallery of the Famous – Château de Beauregard.
Photo Hervé Champollion.

developed fairs - Lyon, improved the postal system, re-established order in the kingdom, restored safety on the roads and encouraged agricultural specialisation in the regions - hemp in the west, pastel in Languedoc, flax in the north…

Charles VIII the Affable

(Amboise 1470 - 1483 - Amboise 1498)
Wives: Margaret of Austria, Anne of Brittany.
Son of Louis XI and Charlotte of Savoy, he ascended the throne on the death of his father. His sister Anne de Beaujeu, on whom Louis XI had conferred the regency, maintained a strong influence over him. In 1491 he married the heir to Brittany, reuniting the province to the crown.
His reign was mainly notable for the 1494 Italian campaign, conducted owing to assumed rights to the throne of Naples. The first expedition began with a long series of victories: in the early stages the French appeared as liberators, freeing Rome, Florence, Naples from harsh tyrannies, then they soon became resented as occupiers of a conquered country. The Italians wanted their removal as soon as possible. After the battle of Fornoue (1495), Charles VIII had to return to France and lost the last remnants of his Italian conquests the following year. In Italy, however, the French discovered a brilliant and refined civilisation. They brought back remarkable collections from Rome and Florence, which spread the knowledge of Antiquity and the Italian Renaissance in France. Charles VIII was planning a further expedition across the Alps when he died after colliding with the low lintel of a door in the château d'Amboise (1498).

Louis XII the Father of the People

(Blois 1462 - 1498 - Paris 1515)
Wives: Jeanne de Valois, Anne of Brittany,
Mary of England - or Tudor.
Son of Marie de Clèves and Charles d'Orléans, he was Charles VIII's cousin who, having died after all his children, left him the throne. He was strictly brought up by Louis XI whose sickly daughter Jeanne he married. From Pope Alexander VI of Borgia he obtained the annulment of his first marriage in order to wed Anne of Brittany, which enabled him to keep the duchy acquired by Charles VIII within the royal domain.
Having taken part with Charles VII in the first transalpine expedition, he started the second Italian campaign (1498-1515) and succeeded in conquering the Milanese whose Duke he imprisoned, Ludovic Sforza the Moor (he died in Loches in 1508). He became master of most of Italy in 1500. He was, however, chased out of Naples by Ferdinand of Aragon from 1506 onwards, losing the

▲ **Louis XII.**
Gallery of the Famous – Château de Beauregard.
Photo Hervé Champollion.

Francis I. ►
Photo Hervé Champollion.

Milanese in 1512 and suffering the defeat of Novara in 1513.
Called « *father of the people* » by the states general in 1506, he enjoyed great popularity, which was essentially due to the building of a healthy economy, the return to a degree of prosperity and the expansion of trade. In the field of the arts, the French, inspired by strong Italian influence, experienced the efflorescence of the Renaissance in their country.

Francis I

(Cognac 1494 - 1515 - Rambouillet 1547)
Wives: Claude of France, Eleonore of Austria.
Son of Charles d'Angoulême and Louise of Savoy, he succeeded his cousin and father-in-law Louis XII, who died without male heir. From the time of his accession, he repeated the dream of his predecessors: the conquest of the Milanese and the kingdom of Naples. He beat the Swiss pike men at Marignan (1515). In 1519, Charles Quint, elected Holy Roman Emperor, threatened France: despite the attempted alliance with England (Field of the Cloth of Gold in 1520), Francis I after the defeat of Pavia (1525) signed the *treaty of Madrid*. To avenge the defeat, Francis, « *most Christian king* », formed an alliance with the fearsome Turk, Soliman the Magnificent, and obliged Charles Quint to accept the *treaty of Cambrai*.
During his reign which made a strong impression on the 16th century, he strengthened absolutism: it was he to whom we owe the pronouncement "because such is our pleasure". Protector of the arts, he encouraged the development of the Renaissance and sponsored artists, musicians, poets and humanists (Budé, Marot, Ronsard, Leonardo da Vinci, Primatice, Benvenuto Cellini...). He founded the College of France and had Chambord and Fontainebleau built.

Henri II

(Saint-Germain-en-Laye 1519 - 1547 - Paris 1559)
Wife: Catherine de Medici.
Second son of Francis I and Claude of France, on the death of his brother, the dauphin François (1536),

▲ **From left to right, Henri II, Charles IX and Henri III.**
Gallery of the Famous – Château de Beauregard.
Photo Hervé Champollion.

he acceded to the head of the most powerful and richest kingdom in Europe. At his court, strongly Italianised and excessively refined, savage rivalries arose: between his wife Catherine de Medici and his mistress Diane de Poitiers, between Montmorency and Guise... During his reign the terrible Wars of Religion began.

He did not enjoy his father's prestige, the major lines of whose policy he nonetheless continued, and also the struggle against Charles Quint, which he was conducting at his abdication in 1556. He died from the consequences of a tournament against Montgomery, captain of his guard, at the time of the marriage of his daughter Elizabeth to Philip II of Spain.

Francis II

(Paris 1544 - 1559 - Orléans 1560)
Wife: Mary Stuart.
Eldest son of Henri II and Catherine de Medici, he gave all power to the Duke of Guise and the Cardinal of Lorraine, who persecuted the Protestants and repressed the Ambroise conspiracy. Suffering from ill-health, he died without children, abandoning a country to a civil war between Guise and Bourbon.

Charles IX

(Saint-Germain-en-Laye 1550 - 1560 - Vincennes 1574)
Wife: Elizabeth of Austria.
Second son of Henri II and Catherine de Medici who dominated him, his reign is notable for the Wars of Religion, between Catholics and Protestants. Catherine de Medici and Michel de L'Hospital sought a religious reconciliation in vain - colloquium of Poissy in 1561 and edict of January 1562 - granting freedom of expression to the Protestants...

Violent reactions followed, leading to the massacre of Saint-Batholomew's Day (24 August 1572), during which Catherine de Medici had admiral Coligny, the head of the Protestants, assassinated.

Henri III

(Fontainebleau 1551 - 1574 - Saint-Cloud 1589)
Wife: Louise de Lorraine-Vaudémont.
Third son of Henri II, he was the successor of his brother, Charles IX. Lieutenant general in 1567, he was victorious over the Protestants at the battles of Jarnac and Moncontour in 1569 and, head of the Catholic party, he conducted the siege of La Rochelle, Huguenot stronghold. In 1573 he was called upon to take the throne of Poland, supported by the Bishop of Valence. He was crowned in 1574 in the castle of Wawel in Krakow. He returned to France at the death of his brother Charles IX in 1574, but he was soon cast aside owing to his extravagance. During his reign the Wars of Religion continued, between Protestants - supported by England and Denmark - and Catholics - supported by Spain. The conflict was aggravated by political and dynastic interests, the crown being due to revert, at the death of Henri III, to Henri of Navarre, head of the Huguenots... Threatened by the League and the Guise, Henri III had the Duke of Guise assassinated at Blois (1588). However, he recognised Henri of Navarre as his successor and was stabbed to death (2 August 1589) by the Dominican Jacques Clément.

THE BOURBONS

▲ **Henri IV.**
Private collection
C. Lebédel.

Louis-Philip I — reigned

Philip d'Orléans — did not reign

- **Robert de Clermont** (1256 - 1317)
- **Louis I de Bourbon** (1279 - 1341)
- **Jacques I de la Marche** (1315 - 1362)
- **Jean I de la Marche** (1337 - 1393)
- **Louis II de Vendôme** (1376 - 1446)
- **Jean II de Vendôme** (1429 - 1495)
- **François I de Vendôme** (1470 - 1495)
- **Charles de Vendôme** (1489 - 1537)
- **Antoine de Bourbon** (1518 - 1562)
- **Henri IV** *Green-Galant* (1553 - 1589 - 1610) *Marguerite de Valois, Marie de Medici*
- **Louis XIII** *the Just* (1601 - 1610 - 1643) *Anne of Austria*
  - **Louis XIV** *the Great* (1638 - 1643 - 1715) *Marie-Thérèse of Austria*
    - **Louis de France** *Grand Dauphin* (1661 - 1711)
    - **Louis de France** *Dauphin* (1682 - 1712)
    - **Louis XV** *the Loved* (1710 - 1715 - 1774) *Marie Lesczynska*
    - **Louis de France** *Dauphin* (1729 - 1765)
      - **Louis XVI** (1754 - 1774 - 1792 - 1793) *Marie-Antoinette of Austria*
      - **Louis XVIII** (1755 - 1814 - 1824) *Louise of Savoy*
      - **Charles X** (1757 - 1824 - 1836) *Marie-Thérèse of Sardinia*
  - **Philip d'Orléans** (1640 - 1701)
    - **Philip II d'Orléans** *Le Régent* (1674 - 1723)
    - **Louis d'Orléans** (1703 - 1752)
    - **Louis-Philippe d'Orléans** (1725 - 1785)
    - **Louis-Philippe-Joseph** *« Philippe-Egalité »* (1747 - 1793)
    - **Louis-Philip I** (1773 - 1830 - 1850) *Marie-Amélie de Bourbon-Siciles*

The Bourbons

Henri IV Green-Galant

(Pau 1553 - 1589 - Paris 1610)

Wives: Marguerite de Valois, Marie de Medici.

Son of Antoine de Bourbon and Jeanne d'Albret, he was, on the death of Henri III, the closest inheritor descending from Hugh Capet. But the League refused to recognise him and he had to reconquer power. His conversion to Catholicism at Saint-Denis (1593), followed by his coronation at Chartres (1594), opened Paris to him (1594): his famous phrase « *Paris is well worth a mass* » is memorable. His re-conquest continued with the taking of Amiens (1596) and the Edict of Nantes (1594) brought an end to civil wars, whereas the peace of Vervins terminated foreign wars.

To restore the integrity of the royal domain, more or less mismanaged during the previous reign, Henri IV had to overcome the feudal lords, restore finances and re-launch economic activity. To do this, he relied upon the support of his minister Sully, whose first task was to raise money - creation of the « *paulette* » in 1607. He encouraged agriculture - draining of the Bas-Médoc marshes and the lower part of the Poitevin marshes - and encouraged new industrial attempts - cloth in Reims and Senlis, lace in Senlis, silk manufactured in Dourdan and the Gobelin tapestries - mainly to decrease imports and increase exports. He also re-launched building activity, having the Place Royale and the Place Dauphine built, and also the construction of the Pont-Neuf and the developments on the banks of the Seine. The building of numerous châteaux in the characteristic "brick and stone" style throughout the kingdom testified to prosperity regained and the increasing wealth of the middle classes. He died, assassinated by Ravaillac, but in the history of France he remains the example of an ideal sovereign.

Louis XIII the Just

(Fontainebleau 1601 - 1610 - Saint-Germain 1643)

Wife: Anne of Austria.

Son of Henri IV and Marie de Medici who, with Concini, undertook the regency until 1617, he was at first excluded from power. Subsequently, under the influence of de Luynes who he left to govern, he

▲ **Louis XIII.**
Gallery of the Famous – Château de Beauregard.
Photo Hervé Champollion.

had Concini assassinated (1617). Richelieu became his prime minister from 1624 until his death in 1642. He was replaced by Mazarin, who the Cardinal had recommended. He re-established royal authority, replacing the great offices with an administration dependent on his power. Trade and industry developed. The main events of his reign were the siege of La Rochelle - Protestant stronghold - in 1628, the Peace of Alès (1629) granting the Protestants freedom of conscience, the Cinq-Mars conspiracy (1642) and the conquest of Roussillon.

Louis XIV the Great

(Saint-Germain 1638 - 1643 - Versailles 1715)

Wives: Marie-Thérèse of Austria,
Françoise d'Aubigné (Madame de Maintenon).

Son of Louis XIII and Anne of Austria, his youth was influenced by the Fronde (1648-1652), which inspired in him a distrust of Parliament and was the birth of his desire to establish an absolute monarchy... However it was Mazarin who governed the kingdom until 1661 with the agreement of the king, who reached his majority in 1651. In 1661 the personal reign of Louis XIV began; he was surrounded by remarkable advisers - Colbert, Louvois, Vauban and Turenne. He ruled as an absolute monarch.

▲ **Louis XIV.**
Photo Hervé Champollion.

Louis XIV is notable for four major wars: the War of Devolution, ending in the peace of Aix-la-Chapelle (1668), the Dutch War (1672-1678), against the Triple Alliance - England, Holland, Sweden - ending in the Peace of Nijmegen in 1678, the war against the League of Augsburg, resulting in the revoking of the treaty of Nantes and the War of Spanish Succession, culminating in the treaty of Utrecht (1713). Despite the religious quarrels, which raged during his reign, Louis XIV, protector of the arts, literature and sciences, encouraged nascent industry and trade. He had Versailles built, symbol and illustration of the "Great Century" throughout Europe - a microcosm where he "domesticated" his court.

Louis XV the Loved

(Versailles 1710 - 1715 - Versailles 1774)
Wife: Marie Leczynska.
Son of Louis of Burgundy and Marie-Adélaide of Savoy, he succeeded his great-grandfather Louis XIV. Six major periods are recognisable in his reign:
- from 1715 to 1726, the regency of the Duke of

◄ **Louis XV.**
Photo Hervé Champollion.

Orleans, then, despite the king's majority, of the Duke of Bourbon (Law's disastrous financial experiment, and rupture with Spain whose Infanta, fiancée of the king, had been sent back).
- from 1726 to 1743: Cardinal Fleury managed the kingdom - the budget was balanced for the first time since 1642 - the king supported his father-in-law Stanislas Leczynsky (War of Polish Succession).
- from 1740 to 1748: War of Austrian Succession.
- from 1748 to 1763: Seven Years War (1756 to 1763) resulting in the loss of Canada and the Indies.
- from 1763 to 1770: Choiseul attempted to lead the kingdom, France purchased Corsica coveted by the English, in order to control the coastline.
- from 1770 to 1774: Louis XV was dominated by his mistresses - Marquise de Pompadour, Duchess of Barry...), Choiseul was disgraced, the treasury emptied and the monarchy fell into disrepute.

Louis XVI

(Versailles 1754 - 1774 - Paris 1793)
Wife: Marie-Antoinette of Austria.
Son of dauphin Louis and Marie-Joseph of Saxony, grandson of Louis XV, he was unable to impose the reform he wanted and did not support the more competent of his ministers, including Malesherbes, Turgot and Necker. An economic crisis aggravated by the American War of Independence led the government to convene the states general (5 May 1789): ill advised, influenced by the queen, Louis

XVI led the monarchy to its fall. On 10th August 1792, the fall of the Tuileries ended the Ancien Régime... Imprisoned in the Temple with his family, he was condemned to death by a narrow majority and mounted the scaffold on 21 January 1793. His execution led to a strong European coalition against France.

Louis XVIII

(Versailles 1755 - 1814 - Paris 1824)
Wife: Louise of Savoy.
Third son of the dauphin Louis and Marie-Josèphe of Saxony, Louis Stanislas Xavier, when king Louis XVI failed in his attempted flight to Varennes, took refuge in Koblenz in 1792, then in Italy, Russia and England. He attempted to mobilise the European monarchs against the revolutionaries. The death of his nephew, Louis XVII, enabled him to proclaim himself King of France in 1795, taking the name of Louis XVIII. He returned to the throne of France following the coalition armies' victory over Napoleon in 1814: the return was welcomed by a large part of the population, who saw in it a guarantee of return to peace with the European nations and the end of the imperial dictatorship. He had to resign himself to the constitutional regime of the Charter, but was hampered by a reactionary clique surrounding him. Taking refuge in Ghent during the « *Hundred Days* », he ascended the throne once more following the defeat of Napoleon Bonaparte at Waterloo (18 June 1815).

Charles X

(Versailles 1757 - 1824 - Goritz in Yugoslavia 1836)
Wife: Marie-Thérèse of Savoy (or Sardinia).
Youngest son of the dauphin and Marie-Josèphe of Saxony, grandson of Louis XV, he was head of the Ultras, who proposed a return to the Ancien Régime. He became king on the death of his brother Louis XVIII, was crowned in Reims and, despite encouragement to accept liberal policies, on 25 July 1830 he signed four decrees dissolving the Chamber with a liberal majority, amending the Charter and suppressing freedom of the press: he caused the outbreak of the so-called « *Three Glorious Days* » (27, 28, 29 July) and had to abdicate on 2nd August. He left France, then after a stay in England, finished his days in Goritz.

Louis-Philip I

(Paris 1773 - 1830 - Claremont 1850)
Wife: Marie-Amélie de Bourbon-Siciles.
Son of the Duke of Orleans and Louise-Marie de Bourbon-Penthièvre, he supported the Revolution and participated in the battles of Valmy and Jemmapes. He was advanced to the throne by Lafayette and the banker Laffitte. Between 1830 and 1840 he had to contend with attempted insurrections by Legitimists and Republicans, while conducting a precarious policy. In 1840, he conferred power on Guizot, who for seven years was the master of the country. Failing to grant the reform demanded by the people, including universal suffrage, he caused profound discontent, which led to the 1848 insurrection. He took refuge in England where he died (1850).

▼ **Charles X.**
Palace of Tau in Reims.
Photo Hervé Champollion.

Succession principles

The French monarchy was hereditary, i.e. the royal dignity passed from father to son, with primacy for the eldest. Initially, however, the principal of election to the crown was the sole rule. But from the 10th century onwards there was a movement towards heredity, with Robert the Pious, associated in power by his father and crowned from 987 onwards. The practice of associating the son with power held by his father enabled the succession to be ensured, which the election principle further endorsed. It lasted until Philip Augustus. Subsequently heredity, pure and simple, was definitely established, confined solely to male heirs.

◄ **The States General of Paris, met to settle the succession to Charles IV, last direct Capetian King, died without male heir in 1328. The crown passed to his cousin Philip VI, of the Valois line.**
Palace of Versailles.
Photo RMN - Jean Alaux

As far as women were concerned, their position was different from the outset; they were simply excluded from the crown. Their exclusion was first of all a tacit rule which appeared entirely natural, when the dead king had a son. Its legal justification was based on a false interpretation of the salic law. The old Code of the Salien Franks, granted around 510, contained an article excluding women from inheriting "salic land", an article abusively extended to succession to the throne. Thereby the queens of France could not govern the kingdom after the king's death, except when they undertook the regency during the minority of the male heir. On the other hand the problem arose when the king died without male descendants. The case arose with the death of Louis X (1316); he had a daughter from his first marriage, but no male heir. It was therefore necessary to wait to find out whether his second wife, Clémence of Hungary, five months' pregnant, was to give birth to a son or a daughter. The brother of the deceased king, Philip de Poitiers, who had become regent, took advantage of the four following months to make the principle of the exclusion of women conclusive. Motivated by personal ambition, he bided by the salic law and the fact that Marguerite of Burgundy, mother of Jeanne, was condemned for adultery. On 3 November 1316 the heir Jean II, called the Posthumous, was born; he died a few days later. The regent Philip, strongly suspected of being the instigator of his death, took possession of the title of king and had himself hastily crowned in Reims on 11 January 1317. On his death in 1328, he only left girls and his brother Charles IV automatically ascended the throne. The principle had already been admitted and was confirmed in 1328, on the death of Charles, without male descendants, the crown passing to Philip VI of Valois, cousin of the king. Also, the exclusion of women from royalty was provided with a second justification in the coronation sacrament. Instituted from the time of Pépin the Short in 751, it was an imitation of the holy unction with which the Israelite kings, Saul, David and Solomon were anointed, mentioned in the bible. In fact up to 1165, one did not speak of the coronation but of the "sacrament" of a king; during this ceremony he was anointed by an unction after having sworn several oaths - in Latin *sacramentum*. The unction was made from the balm of the Holy Ampoule, brought from Heaven, according to legend, by a dove during the baptism of Clovis. The balm, solidified, was extracted from the ampoule with a golden needle then mixed with Episcopal consecration chrism. The miraculous oil served as a sacrament for the kings of France from 496 to 1825, with the exception of Henri IV, who was crowned at Chartres (1594) with the oil from the ampoule of Marmoutiers, usually reserved for anointing the Dukes of Aquitaine.

▲ **Coronation of Louis XV.**
Louvre Museum. Photo RMN - Arnaudet.

Although it conferred a divine character on the king, the unction as a counterpart gave him certain obligations. It included him in the hierarchy of the church, whereby he became a total servitor, with the rank of deacon, sub-deacon and canon. The king of France was thereby canon of a number of cathedrals (Lyon, Le Mans, Montpellier, Saint-Pol-de-Léon, Lodève...). At the time of imperial coronations in Rome, the Emperor had to fulfil the function of deacon by reading the Gospel and the King of France that of sub-deacon by reading the Epistles.

The ecclesiastical service therefore partially explains the exclusion of women from the throne of France, because they cannot fulfil priestly functions. They can certainly participate in their husbands' royalty, but without the power to accede to the throne in person.

It is easier to understand these succession practices by remembering that for a long time, the inferiority of women was generally admitted, and the Church itself had difficulty in granting the sacrament to a woman since until the Council of Trent (1545-1563) it considered that the woman had no soul. The claim « *mulier tota in utero* » - the woman is totally comprised within her uterus - made it clear what the role of women was, including the wife of the king: to ensure the descendants.

Royal wives and Queens of France

Granting eminence to the kings, the history of France has remained more reticent on the subject of their wives, even if some of them, such as Clotide, Eleanor of Aquitaine, Catherine of Medici, Anne of Austria, owing to their personal qualities or particular circumstances, played a decisive role for royalty. The following pages provide a simplified genealogy of royal wives or Queens of France, using the known or supposed date of their marriage as chronological reference.

Basine of Thuringia (? - ? *)
She married Childeric I in 463 and gave birth to Clovis.

Clotilde *(475 - Tours 545)*
Daughter of Chilperic, king of the Burgundians, she married Clovis in 493 and gave birth to Clotaire I the Old.

Chunsène *(? - ?)*
She is known as the first wife of Clotaire I.

Gondioque *(? - ?)*
Known as the second wife of Clotaire I.

Ingonde *(? - ?)*
Known as the third wife of Clotaire I.

Arégonde *(? - ?)*
Known as the fourth wife of Clotaire I.

Radegonde *(Thuringia 519 - Poitiers 587)*
Frankish queen, she is known as the fifth wife of Clotaire I whom she married in 538.

Vultrade *(? - ?)*
Lombard princess, she is known as the sixth wife of Clotaire I.

Haldetrude *(? - ?)*
Known as the first wife of Clotaire II.

Bertrude (or Bertrade) *(? - 620)*
Second wife of Clotaire II, she bore Dagobert I.

Sichilde (or Sicheut) *(? - ?)*
Known as the third wife of Clotaire II.

▼ **Anne of Austria and her son, the future Louis XIV. During the Dauphin's childhood, Louis XIII's wife was Regent of the Kingdom.**
Versailles and Trianon palaces. Photo RMN.

* Note: the two years shown correspond to the year of birth and death.

Gomotrude (or Gomatrude) *(? - ?)*
Married Dagobert I in 626 and was repudiated in 629.

Nantilde (or Nantechilde) *(610 - 642)*
Married Dagobert I in 629 and gave birth to Clovis II.

Ragnetrude (or Raintrude) *(? - ?)*
Wife of Dagobert I in 630.

Bathilde *(? - Chelles 680)*
Married Clovis II in 651 and bore Clotaire III, Thierry III and Childeric II.

Bilichilde *(? - 675)*
Married Childeric II in 668.

Clotilde *(? - 691)*
Married Thierry III in 675 and bore Clovis III and Childebert III.

Tanaquille *(? - 696)*
Known as the wife of Clovis III.

Edonne *(? - ?)*
Known as the wife of Childebert III.

Gisele *(? - ?)*
Known as the wife of Childeric III.

Rotrude (or Chrotrud) *(? - 724)*
Known as the first wife of Charles Martel.

Swanahilde or Sonichilde *(? - ?)*
From the family of the Dukes of Bavaria, known as the second wife of Charles Martel.

Berthe (or Bertrade) de Laon
called *Big Foot (719 - Choisy-au-Bac 783)*
Daughter of Caribert, Count of Laon, married Pépin the Short and bore Charlemagne and Carloman.

Himiltrude *(? - ?)*
Known as the first wife of Charlemagne.

Désirade *(? - ?)*
Daughter of Didier, King of the Lombards, married Charlemagne in 770 and was repudiated in 771.

Hildegarde *(758 - 783)*
Daughter of Hildebrand, Count of Swabia, married Charlemagne in 771 and bore Louis I the Debonair.

Fastrade *(? - 794)*
Daughter of Radulf, Count of Frankonia, married Charlemagne in 783.

Liutgarde *(? - 800)*
Married Charlemagne around 795.

Madelgarde *(? - ?)*
Known as the sixth wife of Charlemagne.

Gerswinde *(? - ?)*
Known as the seventh wife of Charlemagne.

Régina *(? - ?)*
Known as the eighth wife of Charlemagne.

Adelinde *(? - ?)*
Known as the ninth wife of Charlemagne.

Irmingarde (or Ermangarde) *(? - 818)*
First wife of Louis I the Debonair.

Judith of Bavaria
800 - Tours 845
Daughter of Welf, Count of Bavaria, married Louis the Debonair (or Pious) in 819 and bore Charles II the Bald.

Ermentrude *(? - 869)*
Daughter of the Count of Orléans, married Charles II the Bald, and bore Louis the Stammerer.

Richeut *(? - 877)*
Daughter of Bivin, Count of Ardenne, married Charles II in 870.

Ansgarde d'Hiémois *(? - 875)*
Married Louis II the Stammerer in 862 and bore Louis III and Carloman. Repudiated in 866.

Adélaïde (or Aélis) of Paris *(? - 901)*
Married Louis II the Stammerer in 870 and bore Charles III the Simple.

Richarde *(? - 894)*
Princess of Scotland, married Charles the Fat in 877.

Theoderade *(? - ?)*
Married Eudes around 882.

Emma *(? - 935)*
Known as the wife of Raoul (or Rodolphe).

Beatrice of Vermandois *(? - ?)*
Married Robert I in 893.

Frederune (or Frerone) *(? - 917)*
Married Charles III in 907.

Odgive (or Edvige) of England *(896 - 951)*
Daughter of Edward I, King of England, married Charles III the Simple, and bore Louis IV of Outremer.

Gerberge of Saxony *(913 - 984)*
Daughter of Henry I the Bird Catcher, King of Germania, married Louis IV of Outremer in 939 and bore Lothair.

Emma *(? - 989)*
Daughter of Lothair II, King of Italy, married Lothair in 966.

Adelaide (or Aelis) of Aquitaine (or of Poitou or of Guyenne) *(? - 1004)*
Carolingian, daughter of William III, Duke of Aquitaine, she married Hugh Capet in 970 and bore Robert II the Pious.
She was Queen of France from 987 to 996.

Adelaide of Anjou *(? - ?)*
Widow of Etienne I, Count of Gévaudan, she married Louis V Fainéant in 982.

Suzanne (or Rosala) of Provence *(950 - 1003)*
Daughter of Béranger, King of Italy, she married Arnoul, Count of Flanders then Robert II the Pious in 988.
She was repudiated in 992.

Berthe of Bourgogne *(964 - 1024)*
Daughter of Conrad the Pacific, King of Burgundy-Provence and Mathilde of France, she married Robert II the Pious in 996 and was repudiated in 999.
She was Queen of France from 996 to 999.

Constance of Arles (or Provence)
(? - Melun 1032)
Daughter of William I, Count of Provence, she married Robert II the Pious in 1003 and bore Henri I.
She was Queen of France from 1003 to 1031.

Mathilda *(? - 1044)*
Niece of the Holy Roman Emperor Henry II, she married Henri I in 1043.
She was Queen of France from 1043 to 1044.

Anne of Kiev or Russia *(1024 - 1075)*
Daughter of Iaroslav I, Grand Duke of Russia and Ingegerd of Norway, she married Henri I in 1049 and bore Philip I.
She was Queen of France from 1049 to 1060.

Berthe of Holland *(1055 - 1094)*
Daughter of Florent I, Count of Holland and Gertrude of Saxony, she married Philip I in 1072 and bore Louis VI the Fat. She was repudiated in 1092.
She was Queen of France from 1072 to 1092.

Bertrade of Montfort *(1070 - Fontevraud 1118)*
Daughter of Simon I of Montfort, she married Foulques d'Anjou, then Philip I in 1092. She was repudiated in 1105.
She was Queen of France from 1092 to 1105.

Lucienne de Rochefort *(? - ?)*
Daughter of Gui the Red, Count of Rochefort, she married Louis VI the Fat in 1104 and was repudiated in 1107.

Adelaide (or Alix or Aelix) of Savoy (or Maurienne) *(? - 1154)*
Daughter of Humbert II, Count of Savoy and niece of Pope Calixte II, she married Louis VI the Fat in 1115, bore Louis VII the Young, then married the constable Mathieu de Montmorency.
She was Queen of France from 1115 to 1137.

Alienor (or Eleanor) of Aquitaine
(Nieul-sur-l'Authize 1122 - Fontevraud 1204)
Daughter of William X, Duke of Aquitaine, she married Louis VII in 1137. The marriage being annulled in 1152, she married Henry Plantagenet in 1152. From the marriage, she had the sons Richard the Lionheart and John Lackland.
She was Queen of France from 1137 to 1152, Queen of England from 1154 to 1189 and regent of England from 1189 to 1194.

Constance de Castille *(? - 1160)*
Daughter of Alphonse VII, King of Castille, she married Louis VII in 1154.
She was Queen of France from 1154 to 1160.

Adele (or Alix) of Champagne *(? - Paris 1206)*
Daughter of Thibaut II, Count of Champagne, she married Louis VII in 1160 and bore Philip II Augustus.
She was Queen of France from 1160 to 1180.

Isabelle de Hainaut (or Flanders)
(Lille 1170 - Paris 1190)
Descendent of the Carolingians, daughter of Baudouin V, Count of Hainaut and Flanders, she married Philip II Augustus in 1180 and bore Louis VIII the Lion.

Ingeburge (or Isambour or Ingeborg) of Denmark *(1175 - Essonne 1236)*
Daughter of Valdemar, King of Denmark, she married Philip II Augustus in 1193, but was repudiated the day after her marriage then rehabilitated in 1212.
She was Queen of France from 1193 to 1223.

▼ **Eleanor of Aquitaine. Recumbent statue.**
Fontevraud Abbey.
Photo Hervé Champollion.

Agnes de Méranie (or Méran)
(? - Poissy 1201)
Daughter of Berthold, Duke of Méranie (Tyrol), in 1196 she became the third wife of Philip II Augustus and was then repudiated in 1200, after Pope Innocent III obliged the king to restore his second wife Ingeborg.
She was Queen of France from 1196 to 1200.

Blanche de Castille
(Palencia 1188 - Maubuisson 1252)
Daughter of Alphonse VIII, King of Castille and Eleanor of England, she married Louis VIII in 1200 and bore Louis IX.
She was Queen of France from 1223 to 1226, then regent from 1226 to 1234 and from 1249 to 1252.

Marguerite de Provence
(1221 - Saint-Marcel near Paris 1295)
Daughter of Raymond Béranger IV, Count of Provence, she married Louis IX in 1234 and bore Philip III the Bold.
She was Queen of France from 1234 to 1270.

Isabelle of Aragon *(1243 - 1271)*
Daughter of Jacques I, King of Aragon, she married Philip III the Bold in 1262 and bore Philip IV the Fair.
She was Queen of France from 1270 to 1271.

Marie de Brabant
(Louvain around 1254 - Murel near Nantes 1321)
Daughter of Henri III, Duke of Brabant, she married Philip III the Bold in 1274.
She was Queen of France from 1274 to 1285.

Jeanne of Navarre
(Bar-sur-Seine 1270 - Vincennes 1304)
Daughter of Henri I, King of Navarre and Count of Champagne and Brie, she married Philip IV the Fair in 1284 and bore Louis X the Haughty, Philip V the Tall, Charles IV the Fair.
She was Queen of Navarre from 1274 to 1304 and Queen of France from 1285 to 1304.

Catherine de Courtenay *(? - ?)*
Daughter of Philip de Courtenay, she married Philip VI in 1301.

Marguerite of Burgundy
(1290 - Château-Gaillard 1315)
Daughter of Robert II, Duke of Burgundy and Agnes of France, she was the granddaughter of Louis IX. She married Louis X the Haughty in 1305 and was assassinated on the orders of her husband at Château-Gaillard.
She was Queen of France in 1315.

Blanche of Burgundy *(1296 - Maubuisson 1326)*
Daughter of Othon, Count of Burgundy, she married Charles IV in 1307, but was repudiated when her husband acceded to the throne in 1322.

Jeanne of Burgundy *(1292 - 1329)*
Daughter of Othon, Count of Burgundy, she married Philip V in 1307.
She was Queen of France from 1316 to 1322.

Jeanne de Bourgogne (ou de Bourbon)
Daughter of Robert II, Duke of Burgundy, she married Philip VI de Valois in 1313 and bore Jean II the Good.
She was Queen of France from 1328 to 1348.

Clémence of Hungary *(1293 - 1328)*
Daughter of Charles I, King of Hungary, she married Louis X in 1315 and bore Jean I Posthumous.
She was Queen of France from 1315 to 1316.

Marie of Luxembourg *(1305 - 1324)*
Daughter of the Emperor Henry VII, she married Charles IV in 1322.
She was Queen of France from 1322 to 1324.

Jeanne d'Evreux *(1310 - Brie-Comte-Robert 1371)*
Daughter of Louis, Count of Evreux, she married Charles IV.
She was Queen of France from 1325 to 1328.

Bonne of Luxembourg (or Bohemia)
(1315 - 1349)
Daughter of Jean I of Luxembourg, King of Bohemia, she married Jean II in 1332 and bore Charles V the Wise.

Blanche of Navarre *(1330 - 1398)*
Daughter of Philip III of Navarre, she married Philip VI of Valois in 1349.
She was Queen of France from 1349 to 1350.

▲ **From left to right, Isabel of Bavaria and Anne of Brittany.**
Gallery of the Famous – Château de Beauregard.
Photos Hervé Champollion.

Jeanne de Boulogne (or Auvergne)
(1326 - 1361)
Daughter of Guillaume XII, Count of Boulogne and Auvergne, she married Philip of Burgundy then Jean II the Good in 1350.
She was Queen of France from 1350 to 1361.

Jeanne de Bourbon *(1338 - 1377)*
Daughter of Pierre I, Duke of Bourbon and Isabelle de Valois, she married Charles V in 1350 and bore Charles VI the Mad.
She was Queen of France from 1364 to 1377.

Isabeau (or Isabelle) of Bavaria
(Munich 1371 - Paris 1435)
Daughter of Etienne II, Duke of Bavaria-Ingolstadt, she married Charles VI in 1385 and bore Charles VII the Victorious.
She was Queen of France from 1385 to 1422 then head of the Council of Regency from 1392 to 1422.

Marie d'Anjou *(1404 - Châtellier, Poitou 1463)*
Daughter of Louis II, Duke of Anjou and King of Naples and Sicily, she married Charles VII in 1422 and bore Louis XI.
She was Queen of France from 1422 to 1461.

Marguerite of Scotland (or Stuart)
(1425 - Châlons-en-Champagne 1445)
Daughter of James I, King of Scotland, she married Louis XI in 1436.

Charlotte of Savoy *(1445 - 1483)*
Daughter of Louis I, Prince of Piedmont, she married Louis XI in 1451 and bore Charles VIII the Affable.
She was Queen of France from 1461 to 1483.

Jeanne of France (or Valois)
(1464 - Bourges 1505)
Daughter of Louis XI and Charlotte of Savoy (sister of Anne de Beaujeu and Charles VIII), she married Louis XII in 1476 but was repudiated in 1498.
She was Queen of France in 1478.

Marguerite of Austria *(1480 - 1530)*
Daughter of the Emperor Maximilian, she was brought up in the court of France, married Charles VIII in 1483, but her marriage was annulled.

Anne of Brittany *(Nantes 1477 - Blois 1514)*
Daughter of François II, Duke of Brittany and Marguerite de Foix, she married the Holy Roman Emperor Maximilian I in 1490, then Charles VIII in 1491 and Louis XII in 1499. From the latter marriage Claude de France was born, future wife of Francis I. She was Duchess of Brittany from 1488 to 1514, Queen of France from 1491 to 1498 and from 1499 to 1514.

Mary of England (or Tudor) *(1497 - 1534)*
Daughter of Henry VII, King of England, she married Louis XII in 1514 then the Duke of Suffolk in 1515. She was Queen of France from 1514 to 1515.

Claude of France *(Romorantin 1499 - Blois 1524)*
Daughter of Louis XII and Anne of Brittany, she married François I in 1514 and bore Henri II.
She was Queen of France from 1515 to 1524.

Eleanor of Austria (or Habsburg)
(Louvain 1498 - Talavera 1558)
Daughter of Charles the Fair, King of Castille and Jeanne the Mad, sister of Charles Quint, she married Manuel I, King of Portugal in 1519, then François I in 1530. She was Queen of France from 1530 to 1547.

Catherine de Medici *(Florence 1519 - Blois 1589)*
Daughter of Laurenzo II of Medici, Duke of Urbino and Madeleine de la Tour d'Auvergne, she married Henri II in 1533. She gave birth to François II, Charles IX and Henri III. She was Queen of France from 1547 to 1559, regent from 1560 to 1564.

Mary Stuart *(Linlithgow in Scotland 1542 - Fotheringay in England 1587)*
Daughter of James V, King of Scotland and Marie de Guise. She married François II the King of France in 1558. Widowed in 1560, she married Lord Darnley in 1565, the Earl of Bothwell in 1567.
She was Queen of France from 1559 to 1560 and Queen of Scotland from 1542 to 1567.

Elizabeth of Austria
(Vienna 1554 - Vienna 1592)
Daughter of the Emperor Maximilian II, King of Germania, Bohemia and Hungary, she married Charles IX in 1570.
She was Queen of France from 1570 to 1574.

▲ **Catherine de Medici.**
Château de Chaumont-sur-Loire.
Photo Hervé Champollion.

Marguerite de Valois (or France)
(Saint-Germain-en-Laye 1553 - Paris 1615)
Daughter of Henri II and Catherine de Medici, she married Henri IV in 1572 but the marriage was annulled in 1599. She was Queen of France from 1589 to 1599 (« reine Margot »).

Louise de Lorraine-Vaudémont *(1553 - 1601)*
Daughter of Nicolas de Lorraine, Count of Vaudémont and Marguerite d'Egmont, she married Henri III in 1575. She was Queen of France from 1575 to 1589.

Marie de Medici *(Florence 1573 - Cologne 1642)*
Daughter of François I, Grand Duke of Tuscany and Jeanne of Austria, she married Henri IV in 1600 and bore Louis XIII the Just. She was Queen of France from 1600 to 1610 and regent from 1610 to 1614.

Anne of Austria *(Valladolid 1601 - Paris 1666)*
Daughter of Philip III, King of Spain and Marguerite of Austria, she married Louis XIII in 1615 and bore Louis XIV.

She was Queen of France from 1615 to 1643 then regent from 1643 to 1651.

▲ **In descending order and from left to right, Mary of England, Mary Stuart, Mary de Medici, and Anne of Austria.**
Gallery of the Famous – Château de Beauregard.
Photos Hervé Champollion.

Marie-Thérèse of Austria
(Madrid 1638 - Versailles 1683)
Daughter of Philip IV, King of Spain and Elizabeth of France (sister of Louis XIII), she married Louis XIV in 1660. She was Queen of France from 1660 to 1683.

Maintenon (marquise de), Françoise d'Aubigné *(Niort 1635 - Saint-Cyr 1719)*
Granddaughter of Agrippa d'Aubigné, she married Scarron in 1652, became governess of the royal children of Madame de Montespan, then secretly married Louis XIV, probably in 1684.

Marie Leczinska *(Breslau 1703 - Versailles 1768)*
Daughter of Stanislas Leczinsky, King of Poland then Duke of Lorraine and Catherine Opalinska, she married Louis XV in 1725. She was Queen of France from 1725 to 1768.

Marie-Antoinette of Austria
(Vienna 1755 - Paris 1793)
Daughter of François I, Emperor of Austria and Marie-Thérèse, Queen of Hungary, she married Louis XVI in 1770.
She was Queen of France from 1774 to 1792.

Louise of Savoy *(1753 - 1810)*
Daughter of Victor-Amédée III, King of Sardinia, she married Louis XVIII in 1771.

Marie-Thérèse of Savoy *(1756 - 1805)*
Daughter of Victor-Amédée III, King of Sardinia, she married Charles X in 1773.

Marie-Amélie de Bourbon
(Caserte 1782 - Claremont 1866)
Daughter of Ferdinand I, King of the Two Sicilies, she married Louis-Philip I in 1809.
She was Queen of France from 1830 to 1848.

▼ **Imprisoned in the Temple with her family in August 1792, Marie-Antoinette was executed on 16 October 1793, after a painful trial.**
Conciergerie, Paris. Photo Hervé Champollion.

Index

▲ **Marie Leczinska.**
Versailles and Trianon palaces. Photo RMN - P. Bernard.

To visit...

Numerous châteaux illustrating the history of the Kings of France. Among them:
Amboise (Indre-et-Loire) : Charles VII and Charles VIII;
Angers (Maine-et-Loire): Saint Louis;
Blois (Loir-et-Cher): Louis XII, Francis I and Henri III;
Chambord (Loir-et-Cher): Francis I;
Chinon (Indre-et-Loire): Charles VII and Charles VIII;
Compiègne (Oise): Louis XV;
Fontainebleau: Francis I;
Le Louvre (Medieval section) in Paris; Philip Augustus;
Loches (Indre-et-Loire): Charles VII;
Pau (Pyrénées-Atlantiques): Henri IV;
Versailles (Yvelines): Louis XIII, Louis XIV, Louis XV, Louis XVI and Louis-Philip;
Vincennes (Val-de-Marne): Philip Augustus, Charles V and Saint Louis.

The cathedral of **Reims** (Marne), place of the kings' coronation from Henri I and the Abbey of **Saint-Denis** (Seine-Saint-Denis), became the royal necropolis with Philip Augustus, completes this account.

Not to miss:
Gallery of the Famous, at Château de **Beauregard** (Loir-et-Cher). This strange collection of some 325 authentic portraits shows the Kings of France from Philip VI de Valois up to Louis XIII and also their most important contemporaries.
(Château de Beauregard 41120 Cellettes.
Tel/fax: 02 54 70 36 74.
Open from 9 a.m. to 12.00 and from 2 p.m. to 6.30 p.m. from April to September, every day July-August, open up to 5 p.m. off season.)

Graphic design: **Brigitte Racine**

Photogravure, Scann'Ouest Rennes

Printed by Pollina at Luçon (85) - n° L98678C
I.S.B.N. : 2.7373.3185.4 - Editor N° : 4533.04.4,5.02.06 - Legal deposit : January 2003
Printed in France